THE
INNOVATION
MANDATE

THE
INNOVATION
MANDATE

THE GROWTH SECRETS OF THE BEST
ORGANIZATIONS IN THE WORLD

NICHOLAS J. WEBB

HARPERCOLLINS
LEADERSHIP

AN IMPRINT OF HARPERCOLLINS

Published by HarperCollins Leadership, an imprint of HarperCollins Focus LLC.

Any internet addresses, phone numbers, or company or product information printed in this book are offered as a resource and are not intended in any way to be or to imply an endorsement by HarperCollins Leadership, nor does HarperCollins Leadership vouch for the existence, content, or services of these sites, phone numbers, companies, or products beyond the life of this book.

ISBN 978-1-4002-1458-7 (eBook)

ISBN 978-1-4002-1456-3 (HC)

Library of Congress Cataloging-in-Publication Data

Library of Congress Control Number: 2018967125

Printed in the United States of America

19 20 21 22 23 LSC 10 9 8 7 6 5 4 3 2 1

I would like to dedicate this book to my amazing family: my wife, Michelle; our daughters, Taylor, Madison, and Paige; and our son, Chase.

CONTENTS

ACKNOWLEDGMENTS

I would like to acknowledge my university colleagues, who have inspired and supported me, including my team at the Center for Innovation at Western University of Health Sciences (WesternU). I would also like to thank Dr. Daniel Wilson for his ongoing support and inspiration. A special thanks to Dr. Miary Andriamiarisoa, Dr. Edward Barnes, Dr. David Baron, Dr. Paula Crone, and Dr. Mary Lopez.

INTRODUCTION

Every successful business must devote itself to accomplishing certain things. The reward for doing so is profitability and growth. The penalty for failing to act is bankruptcy.

Call these things mandates, if you will.

The number one mandate for every business is to *make a profit*.

No matter what else you do, if you don't make a profit, sooner or later no one will lend you any more money, your suppliers will demand payment, and the bank will padlock your front door.

Making a profit is nonnegotiable.

There are other mandates, all of which contribute to success.

Growth is a mandate. If your business doesn't grow, it will be left behind.

Quality is a mandate. You must make the highest-quality product or offer the highest-quality service you can. You must do this because you have your own standards of professionalism, and because your competitors are relentlessly striving to improve their own performances.

Value is a mandate. Your business must provide more benefit per dollar than your competitor.

Knowing what your customer craves is a mandate. You do this by engaging with them and connecting with them across a multitude of channels.

Depending on your industry, there may be other mandates, such as sustainability or transparency.

These are the things you absolutely *must do* to stay in business.

This book is about one more mandate, which is just as important as the ones that have been long established.

It's the Innovation Mandate.

To be blunt: if your organization doesn't innovate, it's headed for an early demise.

This is because right now, today, we are experiencing two business conditions that we have never seen before:

1) The *rate of change* in business and technology is accelerating. For example, a solution or innovation that twenty years ago might have had a useful life of two years now has a life of six months. The innovation cycle time has sped up, and with it the amount of resources and human energy you and your organization need to invest in keeping ahead of the pack.

2) The *severity of disruption* is increasing. The life span of the average company will soon be on par with that of a fruit fly. This is because the disruptive forces that can obliterate a company are more powerful than ever before. Analyses of the S&P 500 reveal that as recently as 1995, the average life span of a company on the S&P 500 was thirty years; today it's down to fifteen. Half of the companies that appeared on the S&P 500 in 2000 have been taken off. Many experts predict that by 2028 the tenure of the average company on the list could be as low as ten years.[1]

What does this mean to you?

It means that while you and your company are currently innovating by embracing new inventions, systems, or business strategies, and you're probably doing a good job of it, you can't take anything for granted. The competition is fierce, and unless you're an innovation *leader*, you're not doing enough.

For example, you might be doing a good job introducing new technologies to the marketplace, but your business systems are the same ones that were used back when people were renting videos from Blockbuster.

Or you've got the most up-to-date human resources policies including flexible scheduling and salary transparency, but your budget is still being run off the same Excel spreadsheets you used when you were in college.

To be a leader in your industry—and stay on top for longer than a nanosecond—you need to cultivate and exploit innovations *in every corner of your business*.

On your social media platform.

In human resources.

In office management.

In your supply chain.

And yes, in your products.

Sounds like a big job, doesn't it? A little overwhelming?

Not to worry.

Believe it or not, you can create a system of company-wide innovation that identifies and nurtures innovative ideas from anywhere, just like you have a system for marketing or budgeting.

The key is to think of innovative ideas as being like little sparks. These tiny points of light and heat flare up in the most unexpected places! The trick is to spot them before they fizzle out—because, believe me, they don't last long. Blink and they've vanished. You need to capture them, preserve them, and give them oxygen, so they'll burn brighter. If they prove useful, you can develop them into fully realized, actionable ideas that shine bright and last a long time.

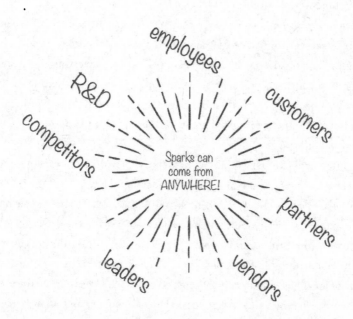

Of course, if you have a research and development (R&D) team, you expect your people to create lots of these little sparks. But even in a formal R&D setting, these valuable glimmers can be allowed to waste away into little cinders. In the pages of this book—as cautionary tales—you'll find some truly scary examples of potentially revolutionary innovations that were ignored, overlooked, and vanished into darkness.

Let's get back to your innovation system, which this book will teach you how to set up and operate. You may find it easier than putting together a bookshelf from IKEA.

This book will reveal the three key phases to creating a practical and durable system of innovation in your organization.

The first is your *innovation mission*. This is the overall road map that will guide your efforts. It's not unlike the mission of the organization as a whole; the difference is that it's focused only on innovation. A big chunk of the book will be devoted to your innovation mission, because it's like the foundation of a skyscraper: it's got to be rock solid.

Your innovation mission provides the direction for your *innovation operating system*. Just like the operating system in your computer, it manages all the moving parts that go into a robust system for producing and exploiting new ideas, inventions, and processes.

The heart of the innovation operating system is your *innovation pipeline*. It's the step-by-step process whereby the sparks of new ideas become bright, shining stars of innovation. If you have a sales pipeline for converting prospects into customers, or a hiring pipeline for screening job applicants, evaluating them, and eventually onboarding them, then the idea of a pipeline should be familiar to you. Your innovation pipeline is no different, and should be a ubiquitous part of your everyday operations.

The effort will pay off! The ability to identify, capture, and develop the sparks of innovation drives growth and market leadership. In the *MIT Sloan Management Review*, Dylan Minor, Paul Brook, and Josh Bernoff conducted a study of 154 companies, which revealed that the ideation rate at these companies and their growth in profit or net income were closely linked. As the authors wrote, "The more ideation, the faster they grew." The ideation rate was defined as the number of ideas generated per one thousand users of an ideation software, which were then selected by management for active development and implementation.[2]

On *Fortune* magazine's list of the one hundred fastest-growing companies, all are innovation superstars. From the top of the list—companies including Natural Health Trends, Paycom Software, and LendingTree—to the bottom, the one thing they all have in common is a relentless drive to capture those tiny, flickering sparks, develop them, and turn them into cutting-edge products or business practices.[3]

Sparks of innovation make companies stronger, and companies that generate more good ideas have more profitable growth. Sparks are generated in a *culture of innovation*. This means that innovation is not just a localized project or a onetime push; it's baked into the very essence of the organization.

It's likely that right now your people are creating sparks of innovation, and that too many of these valuable embers are being allowed to fade away into darkness. It's time to capture them, let them burn bright, and reap the benefits they will bring to you, your company, and your customers. This book will show you how to make innovation an everyday part of your entire organization and leverage its power for sustained growth and profits.

THOSE LITTLE SPARKS ARE WORTH MONEY!

B ecause this is a book about innovation, and the word itself has been used and overused by every business consultant on the planet, let's begin by agreeing on a definition. You may have your own, which is fine. This is not a one-size-fits-all book. The only goal is to encourage you to *think* and *challenge yourself.*

Let's define innovation as:

The creation of new value that serves your
organization's mission and customer.

Innovation begins with the spark of *any* new idea or process from *anywhere*—the scientist in the laboratory, the marketing manager, the techie in IT, the assembly line worker, the maid who cleans the hotel rooms. This new idea or process—large or small, planned or a lucky accident—is then evaluated against a simple standard: Will it add value, help us fulfill our mission, and serve our customer?

Can it . . .

- Increase sales and profits?
- Expand our market?
- Deliver more value to our customers?
- Raise the productivity of our employees?
- Reduce our operating expenses?
- Position us as industry leaders?

If the answer is yes to any of the above questions, the idea is worthy of serious consideration. The spark should be given oxygen, developed, and put to the test.

If the answer is no to all the questions, the little spark should be left to fizzle out. (It sounds cruel, but business is a tough world where you make hard choices.)

It's that simple!

DON'T BE A ONE-HIT WONDER

Too often, we've seen a company make a spectacular innovative breakthrough, ride the wave of success for a year or two, and then go bankrupt or get sold for pennies on the dollar. These companies are one-hit wonders. They don't understand the Innovation Mandate. If it's your goal to make a few quick bucks by going this route, this book isn't for you. Please give it to a friend.

On the other hand, if you're a leader who wants to build a successful business that stays on top year after year, then read on!

All across the globe, the Innovation Mandate is taking hold. Innovation can be big and exciting or incremental and subtle. It can be accomplished by people at all levels, from a dedicated research and development technician who invents a new product to a marketing manager who figures out a new way to leverage social media.

Consistent innovation is not merely a good thing or a useful thing. In today's time of massive market disruption, intensifying global competition, and rapid technological and social change, an organizational commitment to innovation is a *requirement*. Companies that innovate day after day are dominating their markets. Those that take a haphazard or one-hit-wonder approach to innovation are being vanquished by their rivals.

The companies that stay on top—like Google, Apple, Amazon, and Facebook—are relentless innovators. The ones that either perish or fall from the top—Blockbuster, Eastman Kodak, Polaroid, Borders Group—have one thing in common: a failure to consistently innovate, year after year. It's true that the ones who disappeared all had their moments in the sun. At one time or another, all of them were known for their astonishing innovations. (If you're old enough to remember the first time you could walk into a store and rent a VHS cassette of a new feature film and take it home and watch it—that was truly revolutionary!) But they got fat and lazy. They failed to grasp the Innovation Mandate. Soon thereafter, death came knocking.

While many leaders know the critical importance of innovation, they forget that *recognition* needs to be followed by *consistent, organized action*. As a survey of CEOs by Harris Interactive reported, "Forty-seven percent report that their company has no team, process, or system for vetting new ideas in order to decide which ones to invest in. Moreover, only a minority report that their company promotes enterprise innovation by providing funding or access to educational or idea-sharing forums, and only one in three report that they have a team specifically dedicated to brainstorming new ideas."[1]

Many top companies understand that when it comes to sparks of innovation, *quantity equals quality*. As a 2017 MIT Sloan study entitled "Profit Growth Is Correlated With More Accepted Ideas" reported, "Looking at 28 companies using ideation management software over two years, the authors found that the greatest number of ideas per 1,000 users correlated strongly with a company's profitability and growth."[2]

It's a simple formula:

Who could argue with that?

WE WERE BORN TO INNOVATE

For too long, consistent innovation has been seen as a mysterious process. Many call it the *secret black box*, and it's what some consultants and business gurus try to sell you. It's based on the idea that an innovation system has to be like the Manhattan Project: top secret, accessible to only a few super brains, and expensive. They want you to believe that only the *secret black box* can deliver a steady flow of sparks.

Nothing could be further from the truth.

The reality is this: unless you are truly allergic to anything "outside the box," *you and everyone in your organization are innovators.*

When you figure out how to unjam the copier by using a paper clip, you're an innovator.

When you bundle two products together at a special price, you're an innovator.

When you enter into a partnership with another company to share a common resource, you're an innovator.

When you see a need in the marketplace and design a product or service to satisfy it, you're an innovator.

The spark of innovation simply means *a new idea becomes reality.*

We too often think about innovation in a narrow sense, as a massive breakthrough that is going to change the world. It's like how Steve Jobs put it: he wanted to "put a ding in the universe."[3] But for those of us who are not likely to ding the universe, we can still have a major impact in all areas of our life and the organizations we serve.

Human beings are *born innovators.* From the day we take our first steps to the day we shuffle off to the retirement home, we're constantly trying to find new and better ways of doing things. We invent gadgets, find shortcuts, solve problems, look at things in new ways. This is how the world progresses! Every artifact of modern civilization that we take for granted was once a startling new innovation.

The key to the Innovation Mandate is to keep those sparks coming—and to know how to capture them.

THEY DO IT, AND YOU CAN TOO

Sometimes innovations happen because of a deliberate effort. But new sparks often emerge quite by accident and are luckily *recognized* as innovations, and savvy businesspeople exploit their incredible potential.

Innovation doesn't only happen in Brooklyn or Silicon Valley. All across America, low-profile, bread-and-butter companies produce consistent innovations that make you sit up and take notice. Here are just a few examples:

- A leading manufacturer of high-quality power tools, Dewalt has created an award-winning insight community of more than ten thousand end users. The company calls it "user-driven innovation," in which direct user feedback inspires the company's engineers to redefine what's possible. By connecting with its customer community to get to know what they need while gathering product, packaging, and marketing feedback, Dewalt generates priceless data on what it's doing right, what it's doing wrong, and where it should go in the future.[4]

  Your organization could likely benefit from a sustained and close connection with a community of people who test your products or services! You can have one too—all you need to do is reach out to them and listen to what they say.

- DHL, the world's largest express logistics services company, welcomes customer ideas during hands-on workshops in Singapore and Germany. Members of the DHL customer community have participated in thousands of engagements to suggest solutions to improve package delivery service.

  One of the many inventions that originated from a workshop is the Parcelcopter. In development since 2013—well before the Amazon Prime Air drone delivery system—it has evolved into an automated tiltwing aircraft that delivers packages to recipients' doorsteps, with minimal human intervention. Anyone within the service area can bring a package to one of DHL's "Parcelcopter Skyports," and the drone will carry it up to eight kilometers over mountainous terrain.[5] Markus Kückelhaus, vice president of innovation and trend research at DHL, told analysts, "Artificial intelligence, virtual reality, and automation are driving intelligent supply chains and transforming the future of the global logistics industry."[6]

  It's a good example of how customers can collaborate with a company's internal innovators to conceive, build, and test a startling innovation. And by the way, DHL has a vice president of innovation and trend research! He's their *innovation champion*, which we'll talk about later in the book.

- British Airways is saving £600,000 a year in fuel costs by descaling the toilet pipes on its planes, thus making the aircraft lighter. The idea came from an online suggestion box created for BA staff. Other cost-saving ideas from employees have been to replace glass wine bottles with plastic ones, build lighter catering trolleys and cargo containers, wash engines more regularly, reduce the volume of water tanks, and deploy lighter cutlery for business-class passenger meals. The benefits? A significant reduction in the weight of each aircraft, which translates to lower fuel costs, the number one expense of any airline.[7]

Employees are a rich source of new ideas! All you need to do is set up your innovation pipeline (more about that later in the book) and keep it full.

- Okay, here's one from Silicon Valley. Originally called the "awesome button," the Facebook "like" button was first prototyped in one of Facebook's infamous hackathons, where employees are gathered together and given free rein to explore possibilities. But founder and top dog Mark Zuckerberg repeatedly rejected the idea, saying it would encourage "low-value" interactions. Eventually, Facebook engineers called it the "cursed project" that would never make it past a skeptical Zuckerberg. But advocates persisted until data scientist Itamar Rosenn provided data showing that a like button actually increased the number of comments on a post. Zuckerberg gave the green light, and it's been a huge hit with Facebook users, adding to the company's burgeoning bottom line.[8]

This shows that many innovations are not embraced immediately; they often need more time to develop, and they eventually succeed because one or more people are true believers.

You don't need an advanced degree to capture innovation and reap its profits. You never know where the spark of innovation is going to come from—or from whom.

Consider Cassidy Goldstein, who at age eleven invented a device for holding broken crayons together. In 2006, the Intellectual Property Owners Education Foundation named Goldstein "Youth Inventor of the Year."[9]

Or George Weiss, who at age eighty-four invented a digital game app called Dabble—The Fast Thinking Word Game, which is available for iPhone, iPod Touch, and iPad.[10]

These—and millions of other innovators—are ordinary people who may be working in your company right now.

You could fill a book with examples like these—but you get the point. New ideas can come from anywhere, and implementing them is often an easy process that reaps great rewards.

THE MORE YOU DO IT, THE BETTER IT GETS

Innovation is like any other skill: the more you do it, the better it gets. If you stick with it and don't lose your focus, soon everyone on your team or in your organization—whether they number in the tens or the thousands—will see themselves as innovators, will be engaged in the ongoing process of innovation, and will want to contribute more to the success of the organization.

Managers at Toyota, where everything is measured, track the number of employee suggestions made during the year. Over a thirty-five-year period, Toyota's culture of innovation has increased the number of annual suggestions from one per ten employees to four hundred and eighty per ten employees. That's a huge increase, and it's because the company culture has instilled in every employee the value and necessity of new ideas. And these aren't ideas that have come from an expensive R&D program, although Toyota has that too. These are "free" ideas that cost the company nothing to obtain![11]

How can any leader say no to that?

IT'S A TEAM EFFORT

Innovation works best as a team effort, with stakeholders from across the business having a clear and crisp understanding of what it is, its goals, and its benefits. This requires that innovation be discussed in a normal human language that everyone can understand and act upon. By creating an innovation strategy, you'll take the complexity of innovation and make it actionable and real across the entire enterprise. By following it and creating an organizational mandate to innovate, you'll unleash the *profit power* of new ideas and harness their tremendous energy to move the organization forward.

BEYOND THE BRIGHT, SHINY OBJECT: THE WIDE SPECTRUM OF INNOVATION

Many people think about an innovation being only a technology or product or some other bright, shiny object. This is one area that creates a great deal of confusion because the overwhelming majority of business leaders believe that innovation lives only in research and development. In his book, *Ten Types of Innovation: The Discipline of Building Breakthroughs*, Larry Keeley does an exceptional job of describing in practical terms how different types of innovations work across an enterprise.[12]

However, since the value proposition of this book is to help you stay focused on a crisp, clear, and easy-to-deploy way forward, let's look at the types of innovation from the perspective of our simple definition. As previously mentioned, innovation is:

The creation of new value that serves your organization's mission and customer.

The key word is "new," which has two different meanings.

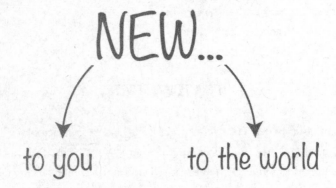

It can mean "new to the world," such as an invention or process that has never been seen before. When it was introduced, the Apple iPod was a new invention. Uber was a new business model. The idea of implanting GPS devices in materials moving through a supply chain was a new process.

It can also mean "new to your organization." Taking a method or process from some other industry and applying it to your own is an innovation. For example, in recent years, automakers have been taking computers and putting them in automobiles to serve a wide variety of functions, from engine diagnosis to communications and security. The carmakers didn't invent computers, but they're finding ways of creating innovative uses for them.

On a practical level, innovation falls across a nearly infinite spectrum of functional areas. This can include but is certainly not limited to:

- How you invent better experiences across each touchpoint for your customers
- Channeling innovations that help you deliver your customer value faster and better
- New business process innovations that help you meet your specific strategic goals
- Products and technologies that you sell to your customers
- The way in which your team collaborates and cocreates
- The way in which you communicate your value to the marketplace
- How you measure and monitor your organizational progress
- Anything that helps your organization either *save* money or *make* money!

Studies show that the most profitable organizations in the world embrace the Innovation Mandate. They're dedicated to innovation as a core competency, and the best leaders "walk the walk" and completely commit to innovation as an organizational priority. Studies also show that consistent innovation—in all its forms—drives profitability and organizational growth and competitiveness, and that innovation is the new enterprise priority.

In your company, the spark of innovation exists right now. All you need to do is tap into it.

THE FOUR LEVELS OF INNOVATION ON THE RISK-REWARD SCALE

Every investor knows there's a direct correlation between risk and reward.

The greater the risk, the greater the reward.

The lower the risk, the lower the reward.

Savvy investors put their money on a mix of opportunities that present a range of risk vs. reward. They want some low-risk, low-reward opportunities that provide *incremental* returns, while also taking high-risk positions that may provide *breakthrough* or even *disruptive* returns.

They also must refrain from being tempted by *empty* innovation, which at any level of risk brings little or no return.

Innovation is no different from any other investment. The spectrum of risk and reward is wide and proportional. Leaders and innovation champions need to recognize and avoid empty solutions while championing and exploiting the next three levels of true innovation.

[4]DISRUPTIVE
[3]BREAKTHROUGH
[2]INCREMENTAL
[1]EMPTY

1. Empty

An empty innovation is something different or new that adds little value *in the mind of the customer*. It may even turn out to be an expensive mistake. If a spark is nothing more than an empty innovation, let it fizzle out.

A notorious empty innovation that refuses to die are those "paddle shifters" mounted on the steering wheels of cars with automatic transmissions. That's right—on a car with an automatic transmission, you can override the "automatic" part and shift gears with your fingertips on the steering wheel. It's supposed to give you the illusion of shifting manually. The problem is, 99.9 percent of car buyers don't care about paddle shifters. As Nick Richards, the product development communications manager for General Motors, told the *New York Times*, "Our research shows that customers with paddles use them rarely, with more than 62 percent saying they use them less than twice a year. When customers do use them, 55 percent say that it is for sporty driving situations."[13]

The *Times* went to a Subaru dealership in Queens and asked a shopper what she thought of the paddle shifters on the truck she was looking at. "A what?" she said. "I have no idea what those things are. I just drive the car."[14]

Paddle shifters are useful on Ferrari Formula One racing cars, for which they were developed. But for the average driver, they're a complete waste of money.

One of the rules of innovation is this: just because you *can* do something new doesn't mean you *have to*. Every spark needs to be evaluated with a critical eye toward its real-life value to your customers. We'll talk much more about that in the pages ahead.

2. Incremental

These are the innovations that are at the heart of "the Toyota Way" of *kaizen*, or "continuous improvement." One incremental innovation alone may not make a big difference in your sales or your business. But a sustained organizational transformation to become an innovation leader, during which, for example, you make one small innovation every day for a year, can add up to real value. In an interview with *Harvard Business Review*, Katsuaki Watanabe of Toyota said, "There is no genius in our company. We just do whatever we believe is right, trying every day to improve every little bit and piece. But when seventy years of very small improvements accumulate, they become a revolution."[15]

It's important to remember that incremental innovations need not be visible to the consumer! They're often hidden from view in the supply chain. For example, consider how UPS keeps developing new ways to shave seconds off the time it takes for the driver to deliver a package. Jack Levis, UPS's director of process management, told NPR that "one minute per driver per day over the course of a year adds up to $14.5 million."[16]

- In the United States, UPS drivers make as few left turns as possible. Why? Results of complex mathematical calculations have shown that when plotting a delivery route, it's slightly faster to make right turns to get where you want to go than sit at the light waiting for a left turn.[17]
- To save time, drivers are taught how to start the truck with one hand while buckling up with the other.
- Slip-and-fall accidents cause pain, cost money, and waste time. At the UPS driver training camp, special slip-and-fall simulators are used to teach drivers to walk safely in slick conditions.
- To save fuel costs, the trucks don't have air-conditioning. In hot weather, drivers work with the door open.[18]

Consumers are unaware of these incremental innovations. They experience only great service at a low price.

This is the kind of innovation that happens every day, and which over time can make a huge difference to your company. If you keep the small sparks coming, they'll add up to a big competitive advantage.

3. Breakthrough

These are the big, splashy ideas that can elevate a brand overnight. Something transformative, like Face ID, the facial recognition system on iPhone. Introduced in December 2017, Face ID is a form of biometric authentication. Rather than a password or authentication app, biometrics are something you are. Relying on the unique characteristics of your face, Face ID initially scans your face accurately enough to recognize it later. Then, when you activate it and allow the camera to look at your face, it compares the new scan with the stored one with enough flexibility to recognize you nearly all the time, even in a wide variety of lighting conditions and if you're wearing sunglasses.[19]

Clearly, this innovation is more than incremental and is going to add value to the product and help Apple fulfill its mission.

Also, it's worth noting that many breakthrough innovations are not new ideas. No one at Apple suddenly woke up and said, "Hey, wouldn't it be cool if our phones had facial recognition?" The idea had been around for decades, and had been done with fingerprint and iris scanning. But Apple made the organizational decision to *make this idea a reality*. They took the spark and pumped oxygen into it. They made the commitment in resources to get the job done.

Don't overlook those stubborn sparks that have been smoldering without ever catching fire. Like the Facebook like button or Apple's Face ID, it often takes time for an idea to fully mature. Your innovation pipeline—which we'll discuss in the pages ahead—needs to be able to handle good ideas that develop slowly.

4. Disruptive

Some innovations don't just elevate the company to the top of the market; they fundamentally disrupt and even destroy the market.

In the early twentieth century, the automobile destroyed the horse-drawn carriage industry.

In the 1950s and 1960s, airline travel destroyed both the transatlantic passenger ship industry and the US passenger rail industry.

The mobile phone has disrupted the traditional telephone landline industry. (When was the last time you saw a public pay phone? If you're young enough, you may never have seen one.)

Netflix destroyed Blockbuster and the traditional movie rental industry.

Online pornography destroyed the print porn industry and adult movie houses.

Uber decimated the traditional taxicab industry.

Amazon destroyed the big chain bookstores and hastened the demise of vulnerable department store chains including Sears, Brookstone, National Stores, Nine West, Claire's, and Toys "R" Us.[20]

The thing about disruptive innovations is that you can't predict them. They're like wildfires that start small, with just a little spark, and only over time do they eventually become conflagrations. Of course, every entrepreneur—including Jeff Bezos of Amazon—strives to be a disruptor, just like every kid in a rock band strives to be Mick Jagger of the Rolling Stones. But few actually become disruptors, and from the outside it's difficult to predict which ones will ascend to that level.

I guarantee you that right now, as you read this, some little company with a crazy innovation that no one is talking about is working hard and growing; and in five or ten years it will emerge as a massive disruptive force.

THE MANY SOURCES OF INNOVATION

In order to capture and nurture those tiny sparks that eventually explode into life-changing innovations, you have to know the many places where they come from and how to identify them.

Sometimes the pursuit of innovation is deliberate and well funded, while at other times new ideas emerge as accidents during the pursuit of some other goal. Innovation can be carried out in secrecy, or it can be pursued with a public campaign. There are many ways forward—here are the key methods to innovate that you need to know.

1. From the Lab

A carefully planned and funded organizational effort can be designed to achieve a breakthrough. The most obvious examples are the new products developed by pharmaceutical companies. To bring a new drug to market takes a huge investment of time and money. A recent study by the Tufts Center for the Study of

Drug Development (CSDD) put the *average* cost of developing a prescription drug that gains market approval at $2.6 billion. The figure is based on an average out-of-pocket cost of $1.4 billion plus the estimated $1.2 billion in returns that investors don't get on their money during the decade or so a potential new drug spends in development.[21]

The study added that an additional $312 million is spent on post-approval development—studies to test dosage strengths, formulations, and new indications—for a life-cycle cost of $2.9 billion.

Another good example of planned innovation was the March 2017 launch of the SpaceX rocket *Falcon 9*. This event made headlines because it was the first time in history that an orbital rocket had been launched into space, landed itself safely back on Earth (in this case, a drone ship in the Atlantic Ocean), was refurbished, and launched again. SpaceX CEO Elon Musk said, "It means you can fly and refly an orbital class booster, which is the most expensive part of the rocket. This is going to be, ultimately, a huge revolution in spaceflight."[22]

In this case, the innovation itself was nothing new. People have talked about developing reusable rockets for decades. But SpaceX made a commitment to making it a reality. They set up the lab, funded it, and persisted until they had solved the problem. In the process, they pioneered countless small innovations that, when put together, made a significant breakthrough.

Planned innovations aren't just big-ticket R&D programs. Toyota's Creative Idea and Suggestion System (TCISS), which was formally instituted in 1951 and now reportedly draws forty-eight new ideas from each employee every year (of which, according to Chuck Yorke and Norman Bodek's book, *All You Gotta Do Is Ask*, nine are adopted), is a form of planned innovation. Toyota has been doing it for so long that the rate of new ideas has become predictable, and while the exact ideas are not known until they're submitted, the overall *idea flow* is entirely planned and has been formalized into the company's operations.[23]

Whether your Innovation Mandate is a deliberately funded effort or a daily program of solicitation from frontline employees, you want a steady and predictable flow of new ideas for your organization!

2. Accidental Discovery

The second source of innovation includes those fortuitous accidents that occur when you're trying to solve one problem and you fail—only to discover that you've solved an entirely different problem. In industry, many examples have become legendary. The pattern is common: the researcher invents something, and it doesn't work; but the invention has some other innovative use, which top management sometimes recognizes only much later. One of the most well known is the invention of the Post-it Note. Actually, Post-it Notes, which continue to earn one billion dollars a year in sales, came about after not just one or two, but four unplanned breakthroughs:

1. In 1968, Spencer Silver, a chemist for 3M, accidentally formulated a weak adhesive made of tiny acrylic microspheres, which were nearly indestructible and remained sticky even after several uses.

   His bosses at 3M were not interested, and the adhesive languished in the innovation pipeline.

2. In 1972, Art Fry, another 3M chemist and frequent singer in his church choir, had a problem: his paper bookmarks kept falling out of his hymnal. He put Silver's adhesive on bits of paper, and they stayed in place without damaging the book. He's credited with inventing the first Post-it Note.

   Again, there was no interest from the bosses at 3M, and the idea was still not developed at that time.

3. A laboratory manager named Geoff Nicholson believed in the idea. Nicholson decided that if 3M's marketing department wouldn't launch the product, then his lab team would market it themselves. In 1977, the product was test marketed under the name "Press 'n Peel."

   Sales were poor, and with a yawn the bosses again said no.

4. In 1978, Nicholson handed out free samples to residents of Boise, Idaho, and 90 percent of the recipients said they wanted more of the sticky notes. Finally, on April 6, 1980—twelve years after Spencer Silver's original breakthrough—the product emerged from the innovation pipeline and debuted in US stores as "Post-it Notes." They were an immediate sensation.[24]

The hardest innovations to identify and embrace are the ones that no one sees coming. They're disruptive or they demand that managers discard their preconceptions about what constitutes success.

And above all, when something comes along that's unfamiliar or risky, the safe response is to say no. There's an axiom in business that no one ever got fired for not taking a chance. In many organizations, the *avoidance of risk is rewarded*. Managers are taught to stick to the company playbook, don't make waves, and reject anything that deviates from the business plan.

In some cases, company leaders are quick to recognize an innovation. In the early 1990s, the drug company Pfizer completed several early trials of sildenafil citrate, but it was not promising as a heart medication. The drug might have been shelved, but male volunteers in the clinical trials reported increased erections several days after taking a dose of the drug. Pfizer, realizing it could have an unintended market disruptor, changed course. In March 1998, the FDA approved the use of the drug Viagra to treat erectile dysfunction. In the following weeks, US pharmacists dispensed more than forty thousand Viagra prescriptions, and the drug became one of the biggest sellers of all time.[25]

Pfizer avoided a common problem: *anchoring bias*, a fancy psychological term that describes the tendency for an individual to rely too heavily on an initial piece of information offered (known as the "anchor") when making decisions. In other words, when sildenafil citrate was shown to be ineffective as a heart medication, anchoring bias could have led Pfizer researchers to shelve the product. But they saw something unexpected and were willing to explore this new information.

3. Collaboration with Partners

An important third source of innovation can be an active collaboration with stakeholder partners. Here are a few examples:

Stakeholder collaboration. A purposeful collaboration among three stakeholders—problem, opportunity, and customer facing—produces a tremendous flow of powerful insights that can result in amazing new innovations.

Some of the methods that help drive the collaborative enterprise include hackathons, the use of enterprise social networks that leverage game mechanics and social engagement, innovation competitions, and targeted ideation sessions.

It's vital for companies to regard stakeholders as partners in new product or service development. As *Technology Innovation Management Review* noted, "Over the last two decades, several studies have shown the importance of cocreating innovations with stakeholders. Suppliers, customers, and users have a wide range of knowledge and skills that are needed for innovation development, but which often remain untapped." Collaboration with stakeholders helps companies learn how to more effectively meet customer requirements while improving performance and development time, and reducing costs.[26]

Vendor collaboration. Suppliers are often overlooked as a source of innovation. As the Institute for Supply Management noted, the most important reason for involving suppliers early in innovation activities is to provide capabilities not available in-house. The next most important reasons are to reduce time to market, and increase product or service differentiation.

They found that while 90 percent of *leading* companies have a structured process for collaborating with suppliers, just 54 percent of the *average* companies have a structured process. The study also revealed that leading companies expect to further rely on collaborative supplier innovation in the future.[27]

Once suppliers are involved in the development process, procurement takes a seat at the strategy table, going beyond reducing costs and improving efficiencies to the next step: focusing on building value and profits.

Brand collaboration. Organizations are beginning to cocreate with brands from other markets to produce an opportunity for the respective businesses and the customers they serve.

In fact, a new popular term, "COLAB," that speaks to brands collaborating with each other, is popping up everywhere. As Alison Coleman wrote for Virgin.com, successful brand collaboration depends on both brands being able to benefit from the existing market of the other, or by filling a gap in the market through a collaborative relationship that competitors could not otherwise replicate.

At first glance, brand collaboration can involve some surprising cross-sector alliances, which is part of the appeal. Virgin Atlantic collaborated with the original onesie designers OnePiece to produce a limited edition OnePiece onesie for Virgin's first-class passengers. This was a blend of two high-profile brands with very different yet mutual consumer interests.[28]

Is there any brand more old-school than Levi's, which was founded in 1853? Yet Levi's and internet giant Google teamed up to enter the wearable technology market. Codenamed Project Jacquard, the Levi's Commuter-Jacquard by Google partnership manufactured a touch-and-gesture interactive denim jacket designed to allow bicyclists to ride without having to reach for their phones. By lightly tapping or swiping a sleeve on their jacket, the cyclist can access a map or change a song on Spotify, for example, without compromising their safety on the road.[29]

Customer community collaboration. As we saw with Dewalt and DHL, another great way to get the best innovations for your customers is to cocreate the innovations with them. Many organizations are building innovation spaces where they spend a great deal of time with their customers and users to significantly improve their product offerings and to create new and exciting customer-centric innovations.

One example of customer cocreation is IKEA, the Swedish home furniture retailer. The success of IKEA's business idea is simple and well known:

- Produce high-quality furniture by sourcing components worldwide.
- Match the creative capabilities of the different participants more efficiently and effectively.

This second part of IKEA's business strategy leverages cocreation. IKEA offers its customers stylish products for a low price. It can do this by asking customers to take over a task that's traditionally done by the manufacturer: the final assembly of the furniture. Asking customers to take over specific tasks in order to contribute value is a key to understanding the value of cocreation.

Are you leveraging the ideas and real-world product knowledge of your customers? If not, plug them into your innovation operating system. You'd be surprised how many of your customers have opinions about your products and services, and are willing to share them at no cost to you. That's a deal you can't refuse!

4. Crowdsourcing

Innovations can come from people you don't even know. While the idea may give traditional managers the hives, allowing complete strangers to collectively work on a problem is becoming increasingly common. With the rise of the internet as a reliable global platform, we've seen the emergence of company interactions with crowds on innovation projects in areas as diverse as mobile apps, video games, enterprise software development, genomics, operations research, predictive analytics, and marketing.

In many situations, crowdsourcing can be more efficient and yield better results than in-house innovation.

Companies, especially established corporations, tend to be relatively well-organized environments for the collecting and leveraging of specialized knowledge to seize innovation opportunities and address problems. The downside is that innovative power may be constricted by preconceptions and assumptions about what can work and what won't work. The ability to innovate may also be limited by the number of employees or other stakeholders.

In contrast, a plugged-in crowd is fluid and decentralized. You can present a problem to widely diverse individuals who possess a variety of experience, skills, and perspectives. The crowd can operate at a scale larger than that of even the biggest and most complex global corporation, bringing in many more individuals to focus on a given challenge.

As Kevin J. Boudreau and Karim R. Lakhani noted in *Harvard Business Review*, innovation through crowdsourcing generally takes one of four distinct forms: contest, collaborative community, complementor, or labor market. Each one has its own characteristics and strong points:[30]

Contest. In an innovation contest, an organizer seeks solutions to an innovation-related problem from a group of independent individuals. The two most important decisions of the organizer are whether to provide awards and whether to restrict entry or run an open contest.

A contest can involve either individuals submitting new ideas for consideration or voting on a set of solutions curated by the organizer.

For example, the Climate CoLab at the Massachusetts Institute of Technology is an open problem-solving platform where a growing community of over ninety thousand people, including hundreds of the world's leading experts on climate change and related fields, work on and evaluate plans to impact global climate change. As the Climate CoLab says on its website, "In the same way that Linux welcomes thousands of software developers to help build its operating system, and that Wikipedia lets anyone edit the world's largest encyclopedia, Climate CoLab enables thousands of people and organizations from around the world to help build such implementation plans."[31]

Anyone can join Climate CoLab's open community and participate. If you see a proposal you like on the Climate CoLab website, you can support it. After the internal judges select finalists, you can vote for the proposals you like best. You can comment on any proposal, and to some you can also contribute if you join the team. If you have a good idea, you can even start your own proposal.

In August 2016, the grand prize winner of the Smart Zero Carbon Cities Challenge was Climate Smart, a software project with the goal to "create a dashboard that allows cities to understand their business emissions by sector, business size, emissions source, and track progress."[32]

Collaborative community. Here, individuals volunteer to solve a problem or improve an existing product. A good example of this is Wikipedia. The internet-based encyclopedia has destroyed the traditional model of encyclopedias (remember the multivolume *World Book* that sat on your living room shelf when you were a kid?), thanks to global, highly diverse collaboration within a new organizational model. The size of the Wikipedia editing community, with multiple people typically reviewing any given article according to organizational guidelines, ensures a thorough monitoring of content quality. Wikipedia uses an automated process to coordinate and aggregate the crowd's edits and keep track of all changes.[33]

Collaborative communities are most effective when participants can share information freely as they accumulate and recombine ideas. This means that protecting intellectual property is very difficult.

Crowd complementors. These are businesses that directly sell a product or service that complement the product or service of another company, by adding value to mutual customers.

The most familiar examples are the thousands of third-party apps you can get for your smartphone. The number one smartphone app of all time is (drumroll, please) . . . *Angry Birds*, which made its debut in December 2009. As of this writing, the various games in the series have been downloaded over three billion times. It's a "freemium" app, which means the initial app game is free, but you pay for upgrades and extra features.[34]

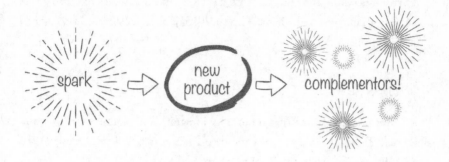

Crowd complementors are nothing new. Back in 1909 when Ford introduced the Model T, the car itself was deliberately kept very basic and affordable. As millions of Model Ts rolled off the assembly lines, almost instantly independent crowd complementors rushed to create a huge aftermarket of Model T accessories. These companies made everything from bumpers (not originally offered on the Model T) to engine parts, brakes, seats, and body adaptations—all to be sold to owners of the Model T who wanted to spend a few more dollars to improve their car.

Ford didn't develop, own, or sell these products. But by allowing the crowd to innovate and produce complementary products to the organization's main product, an organization can increase demand for that main product. For example, you're more likely to buy a particular phone if you know it will work with all of your favorite apps.

In this model, intellectual property may be protected by API (application programming interfaces) and developer agreements. This model has become familiar with the App Store, and it is most effective when a high variety and quantity of complements creates value for the core product.

Although this type of crowdsourcing can be difficult to manage, understanding the purpose and best use can direct the risk management team to successfully implement this solution.

Crowd labor markets. This is where you enlist the talents of self-employed freelance workers to solve a problem or do a job. You do this by accessing a third-party intermediary such as Upwork, Guru, Clickworker, ShortTask, Samasource, Freelancer, and CloudCrowd. These highly flexible platforms serve as spot markets, matching skills to tasks. They have become big business: based in Mountain View and San Francisco, California, Upwork has twelve million registered freelancers and five million registered clients. Three million jobs are posted annually, worth a total of $1 billion.[35]

5. Open Innovation

Open innovation requires that innovators integrate their ideas, expertise, and skills with those of others outside the organization to deliver the result to the marketplace, using the most effective means possible.

A simple example is the buying or licensing of processes or inventions (patents) from other companies. In this case, innovation is brought into the company from an external source. Open innovation can also flow the other way. Companies can commercialize internal ideas by using channels outside of their current businesses. These may include startup companies financed and staffed with some of the company's own personnel, or licensing agreements, where a technology that the company isn't using is licensed to an outside firm that may even be a competitor.

Excess capacity can be offered to customers. For example, Amazon Web Services (AWS) is a subsidiary of Amazon that provides on-demand cloud-computing platforms to individuals, companies, and governments, on a paid subscription basis. The idea originated in late 2003, when Amazon engineers Chris Pinkham and Benjamin Black proposed selling access to virtual servers as a service, allowing the company to generate revenue from the new infrastructure investment.[36]

Companies can also use open innovation tools. Numerous open innovation service providers offer both sophisticated models of assistance and simple websites to post ideas. Players in this arena include such names as NineSigma, InnoCentive, the InnovationXchange, and Planet Eureka.

For example, Sealed Air Corporation is a packaging company known for brands including Cryovac food packaging, Bubble Wrap cushioning, and Diversey cleaning and hygiene. They have an in-house R&D team, but they also work with NineSigma, a company that designs and manages open innovation solutions for organizations in the public, private, and nonprofit sectors.

As Blaine Childress, Sealed Air research scientist and coordinator of the firm's open innovation efforts, told *IndustryWeek*, the company's marketing people identified the need for a special valve for a package. Internal R&D people worked to develop a solution, but given the number of technical, timing, and cost issues, "they just really weren't able to quite get there in the time frame that was needed," said Childress. "People were becoming more and more loaded with other problems with short timelines."[37]

The company made the decision to post the problem to the NineSigma global solver network. They got a dozen responses from all over the world. They reviewed them, and within nine months the company had a solution they could use.

To fulfill the Innovation Mandate, you don't have to have a bunch of scientists working in a secret laboratory deep within the bowels of your headquarters. You can harness outside ideas to advance your own organization. All it takes is a little imagination and planning.

INNOVATE . . . WITH SAND!

Recently, our team spent time working with a client who was the CEO of a big company that sold construction aggregates—basically, sand and gravel.

Yes, sand and gravel. It's a ubiquitous commodity. There's not much you can do to improve the product. The stuff hasn't changed since they built the pyramids.

The CEO, whom we'll call John, wasn't happy with his margins. Every year, it was getting more difficult to turn a profit. Demand was good, but his costs were creeping inexorably higher. Fuel and labor costs were the two biggest problems.

We said to John, "You need to innovate. Stay ahead of the curve. Take a fresh look at every area of your operation."

"Innovate?" he replied. "Do you mean invent a new type of rock? I don't think so. My customers in the construction industry are very specific about what they want. I sell granular subbase, pea gravel, crushed stone, quarry process, riprap stone. Period. It's all by the book."

We understood what he meant. But we explained that innovation isn't just about new inventions. In fact, the vast majority of innovations have nothing to do with products. Organizations innovate in countless ways. They improve their supply chain, or their human resources policies, or their marketing campaigns. Sometimes they transform the company's management structure. Or they explore a new way to use a ubiquitous product and sell it into a new market.

"Okay," he said. He was curious—a good sign.

"How do you ship your product over long distances?" we asked him. "Say, a few hundred miles along the coast?"

"We use oceangoing commodity vessels, like everyone else. Or we use trucks. They cost a fortune, but what can you do?" He shrugged.

"You can innovate, just like the Norwegian chemicals group Yara."

"What are they doing?"

"To haul their fertilizer," we said, "the company is building an autonomous, battery-powered container ship. By the year 2020, it will be able to operate without a human crew. The new vessel, named the *Yara Birkeland*, will replace forty thousand diesel truck journeys the company makes hauling fertilizer from its plant to ports every year."[38]

"Really? It will sail itself?"

"Along the coastline, yes. There are many other innovations happening in global cargo supply chains. In Europe, a collaborative multinational project is creating a fleet of self-driving trucks that will transport goods from ports to destinations inland. In Singapore, one of the world's busiest ports, autonomous trucks haul containers between terminals. Rolls-Royce is developing what it calls 'intelligent ships' that will be ready for service by the year 2020. Big innovations in the transportation of heavy cargo are happening—and you should be a part of it!"[39]

John developed a new attitude about innovation. He realized that even though he was in the construction aggregates business, he had many opportunities to leverage new technology and new business approaches to boost revenues and trim costs. While the sand he sold was the same stuff used to make concrete in ancient Rome, *how* he sold it made a huge difference in his ability to serve his customers, deliver value, and make a profit.

He embraced the Innovation Mandate.

1. **Know your mission.**

   If your organizational mission is out of date or you don't have one, get it updated or written, and approved. You can only evaluate new ideas if you have a clear set of values to compare them to. Your mission helps determine which sparks are useful and which ones you should ignore.

2. **Understand the true nature of innovation.**

   Innovation takes many forms, and comes naturally to human beings. It's not a mysterious black box that's understood only by super-brains or fancy consultants. Sparks can fly from any area of your organization, from the boardroom to the loading dock.

3. **Recognize the value of sustained innovation, whether it's planned or spontaneous.**

   New ideas can either *save money* or *make money*. They are the lifeblood of any company. Whether they're incremental, breakthrough, or disruptive, you need to keep the pipeline flowing, because your competitors surely are.

4. **Make the commitment.**

   Don't rely on luck or happenstance! Your Innovation Mandate needs to be sustained, evaluated, funded as necessary, and part of your long-term strategy for success. Even incremental innovation, when pursued consistently over the long term, can produce startling results and keep your company at the forefront. You can't afford not to do it!

MAKE INNOVATION REAL

I n the first chapter we saw that innovation, defined as *the creation of new value that serves your organization's mission and customer*, must be woven into the fabric of the organization and sustained over time. In order to survive and prosper, your organization needs to innovate consistently and methodically. There are many ways to do it—you need to find the methods that work best for your company.

Having laid the groundwork, now is the time to take action and embrace the Innovation Mandate in your organization.

Luckily, human beings are born innovators—so you're already halfway there. And you probably have pockets of innovation happening right now in your company. That's good!

But you want consistency and quality. As a leader, it's your job to set up a *system* to take your employees' sparks and collect them, evaluate them, and treat them as potential assets. To exploit their profit potential, selected innovations need to be transformed from *theory* to *reality*.

This transformation will not happen on its own or by accident. Profiting from innovation takes a structured effort.

Unfortunately, too many sparks of innovation are ignored, overlooked, or allowed to get cold and die. Sometimes they seem attractive when first proposed, but there's no will or process to take the first small spark and turn it into real energy.

Any reluctance to hammer out the details is insidious and dangerous to organizational success. To win at innovation you first need to build leadership skills that drive innovation as a core competency, while making innovation understandable to each and every stakeholder across the enterprise. To make your plan to foster and encourage innovation easy to understand and remember, our team created a simple acronym. The REAL method consists of the following:

review + encourage + act + lead

Let's examine this concept in detail.

REVIEW

Leaders who become enamored with the idea of innovation often plunge ahead pell-mell without ensuring that their organization is ready to embrace a culture of sustained innovation. If they do this, they run the risk that the spark will fall on damp wood and fail to ignite. This is not the outcome you want.

Without a robust innovation operating system, things like hosting quarterly hackathons, buying Ping-Pong tables, making an unused room into an "innovation lab," installing whiteboards, and making jeans acceptable work attire are nothing more than quick-fix solutions. Leaders sometimes see these measures and become convinced they're ready for innovation when, in fact, the critical ingredients for sustained, profitable innovation are missing.

The Two Critical Questions

The first question to ask is, "As the leader, am I personally ready to embrace new ideas that can be shown to have merit and are worth investing in?"

The answer needs to be, "Yes, I'm ready."

The second question is, "Are our employees in a psychological place where they will trust leadership to treat their new ideas with respect? Will they respond to our call for innovation and new ideas, or think it's a ploy?"

Again, the answer needs to be, "Yes, they're ready."

Fractional, piecemeal innovation initiatives aren't enough. To fully leverage the Innovation Mandate, you need to review the current state of the business before designing an innovation operating system touching every corner of the organization and providing a step-by-step template aimed at building profit power. This should be done with input and ownership from all levels and across all business units.

Your Innovation Mandate needs a clear direction. Set goals, both large and small, long term and short term. For any type of innovation—from saving time in a process to improving a product—identify what you want to achieve, how long you have to get it accomplished, and what constitutes success.

ENCOURAGE

After an organization builds out a credible innovation strategy, leaders need to approve, endorse, and fund the systems and tools necessary for successful execution. In other words, the formation and acceptance of a theory must be followed by clear directives supported by leadership.

Leaders are the key players in fostering a culture of innovation, including modeling behaviors to ensure that the walk matches the talk. Because failure is a built-in component of innovation, this can often mean showing support for untested, new, or disruptive ideas. It's imperative that leaders consistently communicate the vision of innovation so that no one misses the message.

An effective Innovation Mandate comprises a range of activities and systems that encourage your team members to participate in the game of innovation. (And yes, it is like a game, with really good prizes for the winners!) These processes are designed to increase the volume of ideas that go into the innovation pipeline. Remember, innovation is a high-volume, low-yield proposition. Put more simply, failure is a fundamental part of innovation. For every ten sparks your people ignite, perhaps one will survive and show itself to be profitable. That's to be expected!

It's no different from the standard project development process that you already know. In any project development cycle, the steps are:

1. Brainstorming
2. Collaborating
3. Planning
4. Implementation

5. Evaluation
6. Completion (unless it's ongoing)

During the brainstorming phase, a premium is placed on *ideas*. Good ideas, bad ideas, crazy ideas—almost every project development expert on earth will tell you that during this important first phase, every participant must have permission to offer any far-fetched notion. When everyone's had a chance to contribute, the inventory of ideas is discussed, and the ones that are promising are retained while the impractical ones are discarded, with no judgment passed on the people who offered them.

A culture of innovation is no different. In the earliest phase, *quantity equals quality*. The more sparks, the better!

ACT

Following reviewing and encouraging, leaders and employees must *act* upon their stated innovation strategy. The goal is to identify, evaluate, nurture, and underwrite new ideas from all sources. Keeping the innovation pipeline full needs to be a priority. If the company is big enough, this may require an innovation director or department to manage and track the innovations that will come streaming in.

A well-designed employee suggestion program, supported by organizational commitment, leadership clarity, and ongoing communication, can positively impact your employee motivation and enthusiasm, your innovation pipeline, and ultimately your bottom line. You can also schedule departmental brainstorming sessions, or solicit ideas during a few minutes of your weekly staff meeting. Some companies set aside one day a month for a lunch meeting at which every employee is asked to submit at least one idea.

If your people need a structure that will help them get started, digital platforms such as Spigit, which enable leaders to tap into the collective intelligence of employees, partners, and customers to find the best ideas and make the right decisions, can help engage stakeholders to participate in well-defined innovation challenges. Be sure to prepare by conducting a comprehensive innovation gap analysis, and prior to identifying any technology tools, you'll need a high-level innovation mission. Innovation is a people-powered process, and while it can be optimized through a range of technology tools, you should use them with great care and thoughtfulness.

Respond Decisively

Having assembled an inventory of new ideas—or, even better, having facilitated a steady stream—the next action step is to evaluate each one and then take one of these decisive actions:

1. Accept it.
2. Reject it.
3. Send it back for more study, which may include funding it.

Remember, to the employee who submits an idea to "the bosses," nothing—repeat, nothing—is more disheartening than receiving no reply. Every idea should be acknowledged within twenty-four hours, even to just say, "Thank you, we appreciate your idea." If possible, the employee should be notified as to the dispensation of their idea—yes, no, or further study.

In your inventory of new ideas, you'll quickly see that they tend to fall along a spectrum of risk (or cost) and reward. If you created a coordinate grid, you'd plot the vertical X-axis with low risk (or cost) to high risk (or cost), and the horizontal Y-axis with low reward to high reward. At the lower left corner you'd find the ideas that were low risk and low reward. In the upper right corner would be the ideas that are both high risk and high reward.

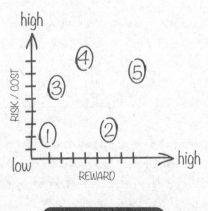

Risk & Reward

In this example, Idea 1 is low risk/cost and low reward. It may not look like much, but if this idea were one of a constant stream of low-risk, low-reward ideas in a program of continuous incremental innovation (*kaizen*), then it would be valuable. Remember, as Katsuaki Watanabe of Toyota said, if you keep innovating like that for seventy years, you'll have a revolution![1]

Idea 2 is low risk/cost and high reward. What are you waiting for? Grab it and go!

Ideas 3 and 4 are higher risk/cost with low expected reward. You may want to pass on them.

Idea 5 is high risk/cost and high reward. These are the breathtaking innovative gambles that make headlines, like Elon Musk shooting a rocket carrying his electric car into orbit around the sun, or a movie studio wagering hundreds of millions of dollars on a summertime superhero blockbuster. If you gamble big, then you win—or lose—big.

But massive gambles can take less-obvious forms, like in 2010 when Domino's Pizza created television ads known as the "Our pizza sucks" campaign. The ads featured clips of Domino's employees reading terrible comments made by customers: "Worst excuse for pizza I ever had," a company executive said grimly, quoting a customer's comment. "Totally devoid of flavor." A woman in a clip taken from a focus-group panel said, "Domino's pizza crust to me is like cardboard." An employee tearfully reads another review: "The sauce tastes like ketchup."

Risky? Yes. Innovative? Also yes. As the *Washington Post* reported, Domino's said its ad strategy wasn't prompted by crisis or underperformance. Rather, the company said it was knocking its own pizza as a way to show its commitment to doing better: "We're proving to our customers that we are listening to them by brutally accepting the criticism that's out there," said Patrick Doyle, the company's incoming chief executive.[2]

Domino's stock price? In 2010 it was hovering at $13 per share. Since then it has steadily climbed, and in March 2018 traded at $230 per share. Not bad![3]

But going back to our risk/reward graph, it would seem obvious that Idea 2, which was both low risk and high reward, would be highly desirable! But amazingly, even ideas that have landed in this sweet spot have been rejected by leaders who didn't recognize or value innovation.

There are so many juicy examples . . . Here are just a few:

- *"Who the hell wants to hear actors talk?"* Harry Warner, a founder of Warner Brothers movie studio, said this in 1927, when movies were silent.[4]
- *"There is no reason anyone would want a computer in their home."* Ken Olsen, president, chairman, and founder of Digital Equipment Corp., said this in 1977.[5]
- *"So we went to Atari and said, 'Hey, we've got this amazing thing, even built with some of your parts, and what do you think about funding us? Or we'll give it to you. We just want to do it. Pay our salary, we'll come work for you.' And they said, 'No.' So then we went to Hewlett-Packard, and they said, 'Hey we don't need you. You haven't got through college yet.'"* Apple Computer Inc. founder Steve Jobs shared this about his early attempts to interest big tech companies in his personal computer.[6]
- *"On June 26, 2008, our friend Michael Seibel introduced us to seven prominent investors in Silicon Valley. We were attempting to raise $150,000 at a $1.5M valuation. That means for $150,000 you could have bought 10 percent of Airbnb. Below you will see five rejections. The other two did not reply."* Brian Chesky, co-founder and CEO of Airbnb, wrote this in a 2015 blog post.[7]

Yes, even smart people are fallible. As a leader, you need to be open to new ideas, know how to evaluate the risk and reward of an idea, and take action when necessary.

Remember, you can't focus exclusively on risk! Over the years, consultants and leaders have created many types of processes for innovation evaluation and management. Most are incredibly complicated and definitely risk centered. In fact, the overwhelming majority of organizations use systems that are virtually exclusively centered around *risk management*. This approach is like playing the game not to lose rather than playing the game to win.

The innovations that come out of risk-centric evaluation and management processes are rarely disruptive or breakthrough innovations that have big opportunities. These types of processes typically incubate incremental improvements. The best way to look at the Innovation Mandate is that it's a stock portfolio comprised of a range of high-risk, high-reward innovations and lower-risk, lower-reward innovations. But you know the rule that risk and reward increase together, so if you want the big hit, you're likely going to take a big risk. Afraid of taking a big risk likely means you will see only incremental innovations.

LEAD

According to the Center for Creative Leadership, "Studies have shown that 20 to 67 percent of the variance on measures of the climate for creativity in organizations is directly attributable to *leadership behavior*. What this means is that leaders must act in ways that promote and support organizational innovation." Day in and day out, innovation requires sustained and powerful leadership. The best innovation strategy in the world will fail without committed leadership. Innovation requires savvy leaders who possess a core competency around innovation and a commitment to make innovation part of the enterprise of DNA and reap the rewards, day after day, quarter after quarter, year after year.[8]

The Center for Creative Leadership describes the three tasks of leadership as setting direction, creating alignment, and building commitment. When these core tasks are centered around innovation, organizations become more innovative and more productive.

Your Innovation Mandate needs to be capable of transforming ideas into reality. Your new process improvement, technology, marketing innovation, or other enterprise innovation needs to be plugged into your organization's product lineup or everyday operations so its worth can be proven or disproven.

This requires the endorsement and support of leaders, because they are the ones who typically control the allocation of resources in the form of both money and time.

Innovation—whether it's a new invention, new product, or new business process—represents *change*. A change from the way things are being done now. If you know anything about people, then you know that most people in their day-to-day work don't seek out changes in their routine.

Innovation Champion

Whether it's for a particular project or to manage a culture of innovation, you may need an innovation champion. This is someone who, when necessary, can get the endorsement of leaders when it's time to put an idea into practice.

An innovation champion is passionate about making innovation thrive within their organization. Champions may not necessarily be the top idea generators or creative geniuses; rather they are the inspirers, facilitators, and connectors. A critical player in the success of the deployment, the innovation champion acts well beyond the initial market launch. He or she complements the role of the project development leader. During successive launches, they progressively develop a keen understanding of the benefits valued by customers and employees alike, guiding those who adopt the innovation by providing them with logistical, technical, and economic support.

THE CSAA INSURANCE GROUP
SPARKS INNOVATION

We often think that creating a sustained stream of sparks is the sole province of trendy hi-tech companies like Apple and Google.

In reality, nothing could be further from the truth.

No matter what industry you're in, your organization *can* and *should* innovate. Remember, innovation doesn't just mean creating a new shiny object to excite consumers of digital gadgets. You can innovate in your supply chain, in human resources, in facilities operations, in customer service, or in any other facet of your business. Innovation can both earn money and save money—and both are equally good for your bottom line.

Headquartered in Walnut Creek, California, CSAA Insurance Group sells insurance to household members of the American Automobile Association (AAA). Each year their 3,800 employees write $4 billion worth of insurance premiums in thirty states. At this venerable company founded in 1914, they take innovation seriously; it's even included in the corporate vision document: "Our innovation: We are building the agility and ability to adapt to—and drive—change in the face of disruptive trends and technologies that influence cars, homes, and the marketplace. Innovation at CSAA Insurance Group means finding new and better ways to improve service, create outstanding member experiences, develop new products and services, and grow partnerships and revenue."[9]

Please note that the last word in the statement is "revenue." At CSAA IG, innovation isn't just a feel-good exercise. It helps the company *make more money*.

CSAA IG recognizes and embraces three specific types of innovation: continuous, sustaining, and disruptive.

Since it's neither a pharmaceutical giant nor a Silicon Valley hi-tech company, the company's innovation strategy recognizes that the majority of the innovations developed by its employees involve continuous improvements that, when accumulated over time, significantly advance the core business. Because they're on the front lines, ordinary employees, from claims adjusters in the field to call center employees, offer ideas for continuous improvements to everyday business processes, the customer experience, and the company's insurance products.

But even at an insurance company, sustaining and disruptive innovations are possible. For example, a sustaining innovation could involve a new product or new customer digital experiences, such as offering a smartphone app. A disruptive innovation would be introducing auto insurance for driverless cars—which is something every auto insurer needs to figure out!

CSAA IG backs up its professed dedication to innovation with real commitment. As *Harvard Business Review* reported in August 2017, CSAA IG provides innovation training to all employees. With a program that provides tools and practical exercises grounded in design thinking, the company encourages everyone to contribute new ideas for product offerings, customer experiences, and improved business processes. The company arranges half-day sessions during which employees are asked to brainstorm about issues affecting their business areas, with the goal of coming up with solutions. As *HBR* noted, this modest investment produces real results. In one session, a team of insurance underwriters reviewed call data and suggested changes to incoming voice prompts that reduced erroneous phone transfers to their department by 40 percent. Another team simplified the process for issuing proof of insurance cards and spearheaded efforts to develop "smart claims" systems, allowing claimants to submit digital images of damaged property for online assessment.[10]

Employees also have access to CSAA IG's "Innovation Hub," an online portal, which includes a variety of resources including articles from innovation experts, self-paced training materials, a calendar of innovation-related events, a design thinking toolkit, and more.

In her "CEO's Message," published in the *CSAA IG Innovation Toolkit*, CSAA IG leader Paula F. Downey wrote, "Given that innovation is the focus of one of our strategic initiatives, you probably know that it's important to us—but how important is it? Simply put, it's our future. In fact, we have accelerated our approach to innovation on three fronts: through the everyday work we all do, in the new products and services we develop, and by putting an organization in place to proactively seek out the next insurance industry breakthrough."[11]

Innovation is the future of CSAA IG . . . and it should be yours too.

TAKE ACTION!

1. **Know your company.**

   Review your capacity for innovation versus where you should be. Get input from a wide range of stakeholders. Be honest: Are you sitting on your hands because your market seems stable and your customers happy? You should not feel so comfortable! Industry disruption is happening more quickly and more deeply than ever, and if you fail to create a culture of innovation, you'll find your market position eroding.

2. **Design your own Innovation Mandate.**

   While this book provides guidelines and key insights, no two companies are alike. An Innovation Mandate that works for CSAA IG isn't going to work for Apple—or for your company. You need to identify and nurture your organization's innovation strengths to match your mission and financial goals.

3. **Launch your minimally viable organizational transformation to become an innovation leader.**

   Don't wait until it's perfect! Remember, innovation is a process that will become an integral part of your company, not a short-term project. Get it up and running. Evaluate it and make adjustments. Get feedback from stakeholders. If an idea looks promising, fund it and demand results. Spread the news when you have a success. Don't worry about crazy ideas—let them go and focus on the good ones. Make your employees a vital part of the innovation pipeline. Don't stop!

3

SMART VS. STUPID INNOVATION

I f you look at leaders of organizations ranging from global companies to scrappy startups, you'll find the attitudes toward the Innovation Mandate vary across a wide spectrum.

Most leaders quickly "get it." They either initiate an organization-wide culture of innovation or they expand and strengthen the one they've got.

A few others—not many, but enough to notice—raise the objection that much of what they see as "innovation" is in fact quite useless, costly, and provides no real benefit or return on investment. They say that, while engaging in innovation makes some leaders and their employees feel good, it doesn't pay the bills.

It may surprise you to hear our response: "You're absolutely right!"

Of course, there are two important qualifications.

First, make no mistake: in today's relentlessly competitive economy, your organization needs to innovate, and not just to *get ahead* but to *keep up*. Failing to innovate doesn't mean that you can comfortably tread water, keep your market share, and glide toward a cushy retirement at age sixty-two. Failing to innovate means the waves of change will batter your company and eventually swamp it. Failing to innovate means you will gradually sink lower and lower until you're under water.

Then, we all can agree with their point to this extent: innovation must be *smart*. It must be focused on tangible results that either boost profits or reduce costs. It can't be just an ego-boosting effort designed to position the organization as an innovator or make the CEO feel self-important when he or she goes to an industry conference.

Innovation must serve a real purpose. We all know the famous saying attributed to Ralph Waldo Emerson, "Build a better mousetrap and the world will beat a path to your door." Unfortunately, it's dead wrong. There have been thousands of better mousetraps launched to the marketplace that have failed miserably. But if they were better, then why did they fail? This is an important point: they failed because they *weren't relevant*. The good old-fashioned hunk of wood with a spring that whacks the pesky rodent is proven, cheap, and maybe perfect. If you spend time and money trying to innovate a new solution when the existing solution is as good as it gets, you're probably spinning your wheels.

As we saw earlier in the book, one of the rules of innovation is this: Just because you *can* do something new doesn't mean you *have to*. Every new idea needs to be evaluated with a critical eye toward its real-life utility. This requires that your culture of innovation has a structure and a goal, and isn't just a freewheeling atmosphere where time and energy are wasted on ideas that should never have gotten into your innovation pipeline.

Your Innovation Mandate needs to be *smart*. Here are the two key identifiers that will tell you if your culture of innovation is smart or stupid. And, no, they don't make a catchy acronym. We tried to think of one, but it just wasn't meant to be.

Smart Innovation = Customer-Focused + Sustained

1. Customer-Focused

For an innovation to have value, it needs to contribute to your organization fulfilling its mission to your customers. If it doesn't, it's either irrelevant or a source of waste. And remember—your customers are the judge of value, not you.

Sometimes it's not immediately apparent if an innovation succeeds in adding value from the customer's point of view. Marketing can sometimes make a difference. For example, in 1998, Proctor & Gamble introduced a breakthrough air-freshening product named Febreze. Based on the chemical compound hydroxypropyl beta-cyclodextrin, the spray was highly effective in removing unpleasant odors from the air. Company leaders thought they had a winning product that would disrupt the air freshener market. Thinking logically, they advertised Febreze to consumers they assumed needed it most: people who smoked or had multiple pets. But after spending millions of dollars, they were perplexed when the product barely moved from the shelves. The miracle deodorizer appeared to have no value to the consumer!

Persistent research revealed a surprising fact based on the principle of *operant conditioning*.

This is the idea that a person's behavior is influenced by its expected consequence, and that people strive to do things that make them feel rewarded. But P&G researchers discovered that consumers who lived in smelly houses were so desensitized they often didn't realize it. They had no interest in making their houses smell good.

Desperately looking for answers, company researchers found a few consumers who regularly bought the failing product. They wanted to know why these people bought it. They found one woman who used it regularly, and she let a P&G marketing guy follow her around her house as she cleaned. Her spotless house had no problems with odors, but after cleaning she sprayed Febreze anyway, saying it felt "like a little minicelebration when I'm done with a room."

The P&G marketers realized the woman was using Febreze at the end of her cleaning ritual as a reward and a testament to a job well done. For her, that was the value of the product. It was her personal validation that she kept a clean house, not a tool to deodorize a smelly house.

In the summer of 1998, P&G increased the perfume content and reworked the ad campaign to show it being used the way the woman had, with fresh breezes blowing through open windows. Febreze became a pleasant treat, not a reminder that your home smells bad.

Within two months, sales doubled, and a year later reached $230 million. In 2011, *The Wall Street Journal* reported that Febreze had become the twenty-fourth P&G brand to reach $1 billion in annual sales.[1]

2. Sustained

While a major product or service breakthrough, like the rollout of a new personal electronics gadget, will make splashy headlines, it's steady, daily incremental innovations—often made by frontline employees—that give an organization the sustained growth it needs.

Sustained innovation comes from developing a collective sense of purpose. This comes from unleashing the creativity of people throughout your organization, teaching them how to recognize unconventional opportunities, and supporting their efforts with time and money as necessary.

The commitment to establishing the right workplace conditions for innovation needs to come from the top, both literally, in terms of leader support, and figuratively, in terms of the mission statement of the organization.

One of the worst things you can do—and unfortunately I've seen this all too often—is isolate innovation in an "innovation center" or "idea lab" that's open to a chosen few. This is bad for two reasons:

1. It separates innovation from the fabric of the organization, and identifies it as an exalted or secretive activity that has no direct relevance to the day-to-day operations of the company. Nothing could be further from the truth! There's no reason why the daily innovations that your employees make, either spontaneously or as the result of dedicated efforts, should be overlooked because they're not a product of your "innovation center."

2. It sends the message to everyone who's not included in the "innovation center" that it's not their job to innovate, and it's something that other people are responsible for, and therefore they shouldn't seize upon innovations when they appear. And remember—you're looking not just for planned innovations but for those amazing moments of spontaneous creativity that can represent the first spark of a breakthrough.

BEWARE OF "POTEMKIN VILLAGE" INNOVATION PROGRAMS

You've probably heard the term "Potemkin village." It's any construction, real or figurative, built solely to deceive others into thinking that a situation is better than it really is. The term comes from a fake portable village built to impress the Russian empress Catherine II during her journey to Crimea in 1787. While the façades of the houses were pretty and freshly painted, behind them stood only rotting shacks.

As you build your innovation pipeline, be sure it's serving the mission of the organization and poised to deliver real results. Otherwise you may have nothing more than an expensive Potemkin village.

Too many companies have shoddy programs that don't help the organization and often lead to frustration and a rejection of genuine progress. There are four chief offenders.

1. The Shark Tank Syndrome

Shark Tank is a fascinating and educational program, but it has nothing to do with building a consistent and profitable culture of innovation that you need in your company.

The Shark Tank Syndrome appears when an organization has an annual event, during which they assemble all their smart people and tell them to compete for recognition. The activity is fun, interesting, and very internally brandable. Unfortunately, it's pointless and counterproductive. Innovation is not a single splashy event, keynote presentation, or cheerleading session. To achieve measurable results, real innovation requires a sustained commitment over a long period of time. Yes, your innovation initiative can include "events," but without the life-support system your innovation initiative is a counterfeit.

To ensure a sustained commitment to profitable innovation, you need to:

1. **Establish a clear direction.** Your organization needs a well-defined mission and your employees need to have a sense of purpose and engagement. Your organizational transformation to become an innovation leader needs to have guidelines and goals.

2. **Maintain open communications.** Innovation thrives in an atmosphere of trust and collaboration. Open your office and encourage cross-functional interaction. Don't obscure the effort by having meetings behind closed doors or burying new ideas in nonfunctional committees.

3. **Make it easy.** Bureaucracy slows down innovation. When Jack Welch was reengineering General Electric he said, "My goal is to get the small company's soul and small company's speed inside our big

company." Stay agile! Keep the barriers for suggestions low. Surveys have shown that official employee suggestion forms that are three pages long result in zero suggestions. Remember, in the initial brainstorming phase of any project, quantity equals quality.[2]

4. **Create a culture of ownership.** To encourage sustained involvement, make sure each employee knows how his or her work affects company performance.

5. **Offer recognition and rewards.** Give credit where credit is due—don't steal from your own employees! However, skip the cash rewards. Research shows that offering cash bonuses for new ideas is a terrible way to incentivize innovation. Instead, rely upon personal pride and a desire to make a valued contribution.

6. **Accept and learn from failure.** As Thomas Edison said, "Many of life's failures are people who did not realize how close they were to success when they gave up." Each failure is a valuable lesson that brings you one step closer to a breakthrough.

2. The No Resources Syndrome

As the adage suggests, you need to spend money to make money. Sustained innovation is no exception. Not only do you need to spend money, you also need to commit people, and you need to have a place, a plan, and all of the necessary resources to make it work. Launching an innovation initiative knowing that you are not going to commit the necessary resources is a perfect example of a Potemkin village innovation program.

It's not just a matter of spending cash; allocating resources often means allowing your people to try new ideas. The 3M Corporation has a long history of being an innovation leader, with a tradition of allowing its scientists to spend 15 percent of their time on whatever projects they choose. Over and over again, it has paid off in significant innovations.[3]

In 2004, Google founders Larry Page and Sergey Brin wrote in their IPO letter: "We encourage our employees, in addition to their regular projects, to spend 20 percent of their time working on what they think will most benefit Google.

This empowers them to be more creative and innovative. Many of our significant advances have happened in this manner." The policy has since been modified—but Google remains highly innovative.[4]

3. The Bait-and-Switch Syndrome

Organizations love to manage risk, money, people, facilities, and virtually everything else. In many ways innovation doesn't tend to live well in captivity and therefore needs to be treated differently. After auditing dozens of innovation programs that failed, our team discovered that they were not actually innovation initiatives at all; more than a few were nothing more than a cost-saving initiative for the company. It's usually counterproductive to tell employees to stop wasting money, so they built out the cost-cutting program while disguising it as an "innovation initiative." The net result is, not only was it a counterfeit innovation initiative, it's not even a successful waste-saving initiative!

It's not uncommon to find organizations using the terms *innovation* and *initiative* to disguise some other strategic agenda. This is extremely unfortunate because innovation can do a great job of helping organizations achieve far better returns on all aspects of strategy.

4. The No Goals, No Measurement Syndrome

Innovation is an incredibly powerful instrument, but as with all tools it needs to have a specific job to do, with a system of measurements to determine when goals are achieved. Putting a bunch of people in a room and talking about innovation and throwing concepts up on the whiteboard looks very exciting, but it's not going to produce results. Innovation is the servant of the people in the enterprise, and its job is to deliver measurable results on missions that matter.

A number of key performance indicators (KPIs) can be used for measuring innovation performance.

Many companies use the "innovation sales rate" (ISR). It's defined in various ways, but most often is a measure of the percentage of total sales that represent sales of new products.

At Gillette, 40 percent of the company's sales every four years must come from entirely new products.[5]

At 3M, 30 percent of sales must come from products less than four years old.[6]

Another KPI can be how many ideas per month you're receiving from your employees. If you're not getting very many, you need to analyze why. Are your employees disengaged and not interested in innovation? Do they have ideas that aren't being collected? Are their ideas being allowed to wither and die because an innovation committee doesn't meet very often and has a backlog?

Your system of measurement needs to include three areas: (1) ideas that have entered the pipeline and are under consideration; (2) ideas that are in process or development; and (3) new earnings and revenue contributed by the innovation pipeline.

Innovation results are not always easy to measure. An innovation pipeline is a system, and the cultivation of innovation breakthroughs requires the entire organization to work as a team. Every relevant stakeholder should be rewarded for both *building* a pipeline (for future sales) and *harvesting* from the pipeline (realized sales).

WHOLE FOODS: INNOVATION IN MANAGEMENT

The retail grocery industry is the last place you'd expect to see innovation, right? In most supermarket chains, it's all about selling commodities, chronic labor troubles, and razor-thin margins. Too often, the shopping experience is synonymous with long lines, bad lighting, rubbery or tainted produce, and surly cashiers.

In more ways than one, Whole Foods has broken the mold.

Founded in 1978 by twenty-five-year-old college dropout John Mackey and twenty-one-year-old Rene Lawson Hardy, the Austin, Texas, chain has become the largest natural foods grocer in the United States with more than three hundred stores in the United States, Canada, and the United Kingdom. Success fostered takeover interest, and in June 2017 the company was bought by Amazon.com in a $13.7 billion deal.

Even under the ownership of Amazon, it's the management structure and company culture that make Whole Foods the supermarket innovation leader. In contrast to the typical hierarchical pyramid structure of bosses, managers, and employees, Whole Foods stores are operated by employee teams organized along functional areas such as cashiers, prepared foods, bakery, grocery, fruits and vegetables, and meat and seafood. Most teams have between six and one hundred members, with the larger teams subdivided into a variety of sub-teams. The team structure is retained within the larger corporate organization: the team leaders in each store form a team; store leaders in each region form a team; and the company's six regional presidents form a team. This interlocking team structure continues all the way up to the executive team at the highest level of the company.

The teams, which are committed to business objectives and the values and mission of the company, have significant responsibilities and work as independent units with much decision-making power. For example, while store leaders screen job candidates and then recommend them for a role on a specific team, the team itself has the ultimate authority on whether to accept the new hire—in fact, after thirty days, the team votes on whether to keep the new person or let them go.

Innovation is encouraged at all levels. As CEO Mackey said, "Any organization that depends on a few geniuses at the top and outside consultants, regardless of how brilliant they are, is at a competitive disadvantage to businesses that more fully utilize all of their intellectual capital and decentralized knowledge." And, "There is no more powerful source of creative energy in the world than a turned-on, empowered human being."[7]

At Whole Foods, trust is the cornerstone to effective teamwork, and trust is built on transparency. In 1986, just six years after he co-founded the company, Mackey introduced a policy of open salaries, whereby any employee can look up the salary of any other employee, including the executive team. Mackey explained to *Business Insider* that he got tired of fending off questions about his own salary, and then he just took it one step further. His initial goal was to help employees understand why some people were paid more than others. He believes that instead of leaving employees to wonder why their teammates are getting paid more than them—and to stew over it—the company should be willing to explain why some people are paid more than others. To an inquiry from an employee, Mackey would respond, "If you accomplish what this person has accomplished, I'll pay you that, too."[8]

In addition, Whole Foods caps its executive salaries at nineteen times the average pay. It's not a new idea; this is what the average executive-worker pay gap was throughout the 1960s to 1980s. Around 1990 it suddenly shot upward. According to a 2017 report on CEO pay from the Economic Policy Institute, in 2016 chief executives at the 350 largest US companies made $15.6 million on average—271 times what the typical worker earned.[9]

What can you learn from Whole Foods? You can learn that innovation is not confined to just new inventions or new products. Innovation can—and should—happen at any level of your organization. It can be a management philosophy, or a marketing approach, or a new way to schedule your employees. At the end of the day, it's all about saying, "How can we do this better?"

1. **Be judicious: Just because you can do something new doesn't mean you *have to*.**

   Ideas are good, and the more you have, the better! But choose carefully. At Toyota, each employee reportedly submits forty-eight new ideas from each employee every year, of which nine are adopted. This means thirty-nine are *not* adopted—and the employees still love the program because they know each idea is given a fair hearing.

2. **Remember, your customer decides.**

   You probably think the shiny gimmick you're adding to your product or service will wow your customers. Maybe it will, maybe it won't. At the end of the day, you need to let them decide. If they don't like it, either figure out how to make them see the value (like P&G did with Febreze) or pull the plug.

3. **Spark an organizational transformation to become an innovation leader.**

   Avoid the Potemkin village syndrome. Too many "innovation centers" or "idea labs" are nothing more than empty showplaces. Innovation is happening—and needs to be recognized and nurtured—in every corner of your organization.

4

THE INNOVATION MISSION

This chapter, and the three that follow it, are devoted to building the foundation of your Innovation Mandate.

This is important work, deserving of four full chapters.

First, let's talk about your innovation mission.

We call it the innovation "mission" rather than "strategy" because your mission includes the most important three-letter word in your vocabulary: "Why?" Your innovation mission is like a military mission, where the rationale and the goal are both clearly defined.

Creating your innovation mission requires clear eyes, tough questions, and honest answers. Now is not the time to play footsie. It's the time to turn ideas into action.

This is the framework upon which you'll build your innovation operating system, of which the key component is your innovation pipeline.

Mission, operating system, pipeline: together they exist to serve your Innovation Mandate and all those tiny little sparks of innovation. These sparks can be fragile things, easily stamped out by lack of vision and poor management.

This is not what you want to happen in your organization.

What you want is a continuous eruption of little sparks and big sparks popping up all over your organization, giving energy to innovation and lighting the way toward market domination. You want both planned innovation and unplanned, spontaneous breakthroughs. You want to be able to go to your R&D people and say, "Congratulations on yet another breakthrough," and you also want to be able to pick up the phone and call a random employee and say, "Thank you for your suggestion! You'll be pleased to know that it's being implemented and we expect to reduce our departmental expenses by two percent. That's huge! Thank you."

INNOVATION MANDATE + GOOD MANAGEMENT = SUCCESS

Remember that while having an innovation mission is the new mandate, it must always be pursued in a context of sound business decisions. Innovation combined with lousy management won't get you very far.

Consider the sad story of toy retailing giant Toys "R" Us. As of March 2018, the company held 15 percent of US toy revenue. With that kind of market share, you'd think the purveyor of plastic stuff made in China should be in a comfortable position, not headed for liquidation.

But the toy chain's US division, which entered bankruptcy in September 2017, now looks like it might be sold for scrap. Massive debt is one problem, but most analysts say the company's problems began in 2000 when they made a ten-year deal with Amazon.com to sell online exclusively through the e-commerce giant. It was a fateful choice, especially when you consider that, a few months earlier, Toys "R" Us had received a $60 million investment from Japanese technology conglomerate SoftBank to develop its online retailing. But then Toys "R" Us changed course, backed away from its own innovation program, and announced the partnership to sell toys online with Amazon.

Under the terms of the deal, Toys "R" Us agreed to stock a wide variety of its most popular toys on Amazon in exchange for being Amazon's exclusive seller of toys and baby products. The companies also agreed that Toys "R" Us would give up its online autonomy, with ToysRUs.com redirecting back to Amazon.

But soon, Amazon started selling toys from other sources. Toys "R" Us sued, and in 2006 their contract with Amazon was torn up. The company won the right to reopen an independent website. It may have been what Toys "R" Us needed, but the Toys "R" Us website was never competitive in terms of customer experience. It was slow and cumbersome, and didn't get any better. They were far behind in organizational capability to manage online sales.[1]

The spark of innovation had been stamped out by dumb business decisions.

As Reuters reported in December 2017, to become profitable the company is taking a high-risk, high-reward gamble, setting aside more than $400 million out of its $3.1 billion in bankruptcy loans for sprucing up its approximately eight hundred stores over the next three years with more customer experiences and better-paid staff. But they may be innovating in the wrong direction, because in the retail toy sector, online sales of toys are growing while store visits are declining.[2]

Time will tell if Toys "R" Us has made the right strategic move!

The Three Cs
⟹ Commitment
⟹ Customization
⟹ Creativity

The story of Toys "R" Us sets the stage for the Three Cs of innovation mission success: commitment, customization, and creativity. In each one of them, the company stumbled. You can avoid their mistakes and keep the spark of innovation alive and profitable.

COMMITMENT

As we've seen, the single biggest cause of innovation program failure in organizations is that they simply took a half-hearted swipe at it. The system for innovation was incomplete and oftentimes poorly contrived, and not surprisingly it failed.

In the case of Toys "R" Us, their history reveals an inconsistent and ambivalent approach to innovation.

They began, in fact, as innovators in e-commerce. And at its peak, Toys "R" Us was considered a classic example of a highly disruptive category killer, a business that specialized so thoroughly and efficiently in one sector that it destroyed competition from both smaller specialty stores and larger general retailers. In 1998, the company joined the online retailing boom with the launch of the ToysRUs. com website. (At this time, Amazon.com was mainly focused on books and still unprofitable.) But the effort was insufficient, resulting in the now-legendary Christmas 1999 online meltdown as ToysRUs.com failed to deliver many online orders by December 25. Then the company sought the big SoftBank investment for e-commerce. A few months later they threw in the towel and signed with Amazon.

Be Both Agile and Strategic

This behavior points to a key lesson: you need to be both *agile* and *strategic*.

Being agile means responding to disruption and making it work for you, not against you. It means being sensitive to change and quick to adapt.

Being strategic means keeping your eye on the prize. Chart a course for the future and don't lose your nerve when faced with challenges. Know your market and how you can best serve it. Know why people buy your products or services as opposed to someone else's. Don't destroy your brand with either arrogance or indecision.

Your organizational commitment to innovation needs to be all-inclusive and touch every person who works for you. It needs to be long lasting, not the flavor of the month.

Support for the Innovation Operating System

When assessing an organization's innovation program, you need to evaluate and understand the sincere level of commitment from the very top. A litmus test of commitment is the support shown by top management for the *innovation operating system* (IOS), which as it's developed incrementally pushes forward in a way that reports out well-defined innovation successes. In other words, every organization needs an IOS that's consistent with the CEO's expectation in terms of expected outcome and overall costs. Once you understand the true level of commitment, you can architect a custom IOS, as you will need continued leadership sponsorship to succeed.

In the chapters ahead, we'll talk much more in depth about your innovation operating system.

If It's Going to Be Yours . . . Prove It!

If you're really going to embrace your Innovation Mandate, you need to commit to it as if your life depended on it—almost literally. Actually, it would be accurate to say that you should commit to innovation as if your *professional career* depended on it. Remember, the two biggest causes of innovation failure in organizations are: 1) an incomplete and fractional approach to innovation (the Bumper Sticker Syndrome), and 2) the inability to connect the uniqueness of your organization, your people, and your market to your innovation.

This leads us to the next "C," customization.

CUSTOMIZATION

Without a doubt, the second biggest reason why the spark of innovation is too often extinguished is the one-size-fits-all approach. Just like people, no two organizations are alike. Even among companies in the same industry, each has its own DNA. Consider the software industry. There are the big players—Microsoft, Google, IBM, Oracle, Facebook, SAP, and others. There are middle players—Sage, Red Hat, Cadence Design, Trend Micro. Then you have the up-and-coming little guys—15Five, Bonusly, Image Relay, Clearbit. They're all more or less in the same industry, yet they're all very different. What innovation means to Microsoft is not what it means to 15Five!

Innovation Isn't a Software Package

Too many managers and leaders attempt to create an innovation infrastructure by simply purchasing a software package. If only it were that easy! Innovation requires a comprehensive ecosystem that is complete and healthy. While it's true that technology can have an important place in terms of driving collaboration across your organization, innovation platforms and other technologies are just one part of the solution. The biggest part of the solution—in fact, the only one that's absolutely indispensable—is your *people*. If your people aren't committed to a culture of innovation, and if they don't each love experiencing the spark of a new idea or solution to a problem, you can buy all the software you want and it's not going to help one iota.

Misguided Companies Create Innovation "Initiatives"

If you approach innovation as this quarter's strategic initiative, you will likely not be able to develop a scalable organizational transformation to become an innovation leader that delivers proven returns on investment year after year. Most so-called strategic initiatives fail in general, and that's certainly the case with innovation. When you think about innovation, think of it as a recommitment to your organization's genesis of innovation. Virtually every organization begins with the spark of innovation, and the successful ones keep generating sparks, year after year. Make innovation part of your enterprise DNA and your organizational culture, and it will provide tremendous returns to you and your organization.

CREATIVITY

It may seem like an obvious thing to say, but for your Innovation Mandate to take hold in your company there needs to be a baseline level of creativity at all levels.

The good news is that creativity is a skill that, with practice, can be strengthened. It's just like any other skill, such as playing piano or using an Excel spreadsheet. The more you do it, the better you get at it, and the easier it becomes.

The "F Word" and Innovation

I hate to be one of those authors who throws around the "F word," but I have to say, in order to make innovation work, it has to be . . .

This can't be overstated enough. Innovation is a people-powered process that can only be engaging and successful when we make it a positive experience rather than another bureaucratic task. When you think about it, the most humanist of behaviors is that of creation, and when we are creating we are having fun. Baking fun into your innovation activities will make the difference between success and failure. As we build out an innovation operating system, we need to create a wide range of activities that are fun, productive, and beneficial for all involved, both the organization and employees.

WHAT'S YOUR ORGANIZATIONAL APPETITE FOR RISK?

If you talk to most innovation experts, they will quickly tell you that one of the major causes of innovation failure in most organizations today is an incessant focus on "risk management," which, translated into normal English, means "playing it safe." Once an organization achieves a certain level of risk, their gaze shifts from a focus on customers and opportunities to a focus on compliance and risk management. This is unfortunate, because you can absolutely manage risk and compliance while still driving an incredibly innovative organization.

In fact, you could effectively argue that the biggest risk to an organization today is *not* taking risks. This is exactly what Mark Zuckerberg said in a rare interview at Y Combinator's Startup School in Palo Alto, California, in October 2011: "The biggest risk is not taking any risk. In a world that's changing really quickly, the only strategy that is guaranteed to fail is not taking risks." Of course, the level of risk that your organization can tolerate is an individual issue, but remember that, like any other skill, risk can be learned.[3]

As you put together your innovation operating system, it's incredibly important that you architect it in such a way that it squares up with the risk appetite of the leadership and organization.

"HI, MY NAME IS JIM, AND I'M IN CHARGE OF PRESSING THE 'GO' BUTTON"

Have you ever gone to an organization and asked them, "Who's in charge of innovation?" In some organizations, if you ask that question, the employee will look at you like you're crazy! It may sound arcane, but every CEO should ask themselves: "Who's in charge of pressing the 'go' button?"

This is because a successful Innovation Mandate always leads to *change*. The change may involve the shifting of the labor of employees, allocating funding from the budget, alteration in the supply chain, adjustments to a marketing campaign—the ripple effect can be very wide.

If an innovation is local, such as one that affects the work of just one team, then the responsible person might simply be the manager of the team. If it involves several departments, the person who can say yes must have sufficient authority over all of them. If it involves a new allocation of funds, then the finance people need to get on board.

In a large company, you may need a dedicated innovation leader who can manage the various stakeholders and ensure that a new idea gets the support it needs from everyone who's impacted by it. Otherwise, you'll have turf wars, which are never good for anybody.

The term "chief innovation officer" was first coined and described in the 1998 book *Fourth Generation R&D: Managing Knowledge, Technology, and Innovation*, by William L. Miller and Langdon Morris. Successful chief innovation officers (CIOs) focus on managing the innovation process inside the organization, which includes identifying strategies, business opportunities, and new technologies, and then developing new capabilities and architectures with partners, new business models, and new industry structures to serve those opportunities.[4]

The words *chief* and *officer* have significance. Using a functional "chief . . . officer" title signifies that this is a cross-organizational position and empowers this person to work across organizational silos.

In a small company, the CIO can be the CEO. But in a large company with many departments or teams, you'll need a dedicated chief innovation officer.

Who's in charge of pressing the "go" button in your organization?

INNOVATION NEEDS TO BE IN
YOUR ORGANIZATION'S DNA

Remember, your Innovation Mandate isn't like the pair of expensive shoes that you put on in the morning and take off at night. Innovation needs to be like your *feet*: a part of your body that you depend on and, hopefully, don't even think about. As you go about your daily business, your feet take you where you need to go. Yes, they need to be cared for, but they're a part of who you are, and carry the same DNA as any other part of your body.

If innovation isn't in your company's DNA, adapting to change will be much more difficult.

As Ron Ashkenas pointed out in a 2012 article for the *Harvard Business Review*, some companies seem to be oblivious to change, while others are consistently one step ahead. The difference is in their innovation DNA. For example:[5]

- Leaders at the United States Postal Service knew for years—or *should* have known—that its traditional business model was being massively disrupted by email. Yet they willfully turned a blind eye as deficits mounted.
- Long before they changed their business strategy, the people at Eastman Kodak could see that film was being replaced by digital media. But they didn't respond.
- Years before it took action, AOL knew that dial-up subscriptions were falling.
- General Electric—which normally leads innovation—inexplicably waited a very long time to shift its lighting business away from incandescent bulbs.
- In 1996, General Motors developed the first practical electric car. While reviews were enthusiastic, GM executives became convinced the EV1 was too innovative and ordered the program scrapped, including all the cars. In the March 13, 2007, issue of *Newsweek*, GM R&D chief Larry

Burns expressed regret GM killed the car his engineers had developed a decade earlier: "If we could turn back the hands of time, we could have had the Chevy Volt ten years earlier."[6]

On the other hand, because innovation is in their DNA, some companies seem to be one step ahead:

- When IBM sold its PC division to Lenovo in 2005, many analysts thought it was crazy for the company to divest itself from a unit it had worked so hard to create. But eventually analysts realized IBM had made a savvy move to exit early rather than struggle with PC commoditization, pricing pressures, and supply chain issues.
- At the turn of the century, Intuit realized that by remaining only a financial software firm it could not continue to grow, and began to consciously create, acquire, and incubate new businesses, which now make up more than half the company.
- What business could be more boring than selling home improvement merchandise, like carpeting and paneling? The people at Lowe's don't think it's boring at all, and have introduced some dramatic innovations. They developed software for store employees to use while assisting customers, allowing customers, for example, to determine how much carpet is needed in a given area of space just by using a picture, and reading product reviews with 360-degree views of the product. Their Virtual Room Designer allows customers to fully visualize a room by setting the dimensions, then choosing cabinets, walls, flooring, and more. Lowe's developed something the customers (and employees) didn't even know they needed, and it's changing the in-store experience for both parties.[7]

PATAGONIA MAKES INNOVATION FUN—AND PROFITABLE

If you make the overall work environment more collaborative, more human, and more positive, the spark of innovation will burn that much brighter, and profits will follow.

Founded by Yvon Chouinard in 1973, Patagonia is an American clothing company that sells outdoor clothing marketed as being sustainable. The company employs one thousand people, many at its Ventura, California, headquarters. They're at the forefront of encouraging innovation not only with formal programs but by making work more fun. Their commitment makes sense, because the company was founded by people who climb mountains, an activity that is both fun and risky.

Take human resources, for example. Since 1983, Patagonia has pursued innovative on-site child care. (They even wrote a book about it, entitled *Family Business*.) As the company says, "Strong families build strong businesses. . . . Providing quality on-site child care and paid leave for working families is at the heart of responsible business." Kids actually come to work with their parents and don't have to be quarantined in an isolated child-care area. As one employee said about having her children at work with her every day, "It is not just making a living, it is making a life."

At Patagonia, play is important. "Unstructured play," the company says, "where kids get messy and wild, is the pinnacle of play; and it's at the core of Patagonia's child-care program. Rejecting the idea that early childhood is for academics, we stand for children's right to play."[8]

And yes, for all those curmudgeons who think this is all a bunch of cushiony nonsense, Patagonia addresses the bottom line, saying, "It's expensive to offer quality care and subsidize tuition, but the benefits—financial and otherwise—pay for themselves every year."[9]

TAKE ACTION!

1. **Commit to your Innovation Mandate.**

   Innovation is just as important to your organization as sales, production, finance, or any other area of activity. It needs to be a part of your organization's DNA. Remember—if you don't innovate and seek ways to do your job better and better, you will fall behind and ultimately perish, just like the dinosaurs.

2. **Customize your approach to fit your organization.**

   Just like DNA, which is different for every human being (even, according to new evidence, identical twins), your company's DNA is unique. While there are clear concepts for creating a culture of innovation, which is what this book is all about, the exact expression of those concepts is different for every organization. Beware of innovation consultants bearing boxed one-size-fits-all solutions—they may not work for you!

3. **Create a positive, happy environment.**

   The human mind is most likely to innovate when it possesses a positive outlook. The spark of innovation can come at any time, and when it does, one of two things can happen: it can be allowed to fizzle out and get cold, or it can be captured and its energy put to good use. New ideas that aren't captured and evaluated are a form of waste and missed opportunity cost. Keep them working for you!

4. **Assign responsibility.**

   Innovation means *change*—sometimes disruptive, sometimes incremental. Consequently, every organization needs someone who has the authority and responsibility to encourage and manage innovation. This could be the CEO, team leaders, or a dedicated chief innovation officer (CIO).

5

THE SIX COMMITMENTS OF
YOUR INNOVATION MANDATE

Question: What's the number one cause of innovation failure?

Answer: A lack of commitment.

This shouldn't be surprising, because you could say the same thing about many areas of life.

Ask any winning athlete about the key to sustained excellence, and he or she will reply, "Commitment."

Ask any salesperson, inventor, military officer, or sports coach, and they'll give the same answer.

Commitment.

Not backing down. Not being half-hearted. Not giving less than one hundred percent.

Your Innovation Mandate is no different.

In our work with leaders of companies large and small, we've learned that the ones who spark innovation and keep it going in every corner of their organization are rewarded with sustained growth and profits, year after year.

The leaders who take a half-hearted approach to innovation, who don't spark and support a sustained effort, experience slow decline and eventual takeover or even bankruptcy.

In previous chapters we've discussed Making Innovation REAL with Commitment, Customization, and Creativity.

Now it's time to drill down more deeply into the many facets of REAL Commitment.

COMMITMENT MUST BE MULTIFACETED
(JUST ASK AMAZON.COM)

If you look at companies that have made innnovation an integral part of their organizational DNA, you quickly see that they've committed to innovate on many levels.

Take, for example, Amazon.com, which in the past decade has become a true market disruptor. Their record of innovation began with the first simple spark of insight:

People don't need to touch and handle a book before they're willing to buy it. Most people would be happy to buy a book from an internet retailer, because the level of trust is sufficiently high.

This simple spark led Jeff Bezos to launch Amazon.com on July 5, 1994.

I'm not going to bore you with the history of Amazon, because you're probably a customer of the e-commerce giant and know all about it. But you may not be aware that Amazon has a long record of commitment to innovation in areas that you might not think about.

Amazon's entire business is based on answering yes to two simple questions:

"Do you have what I want?"

"Can you get it to me when I need it?"

Every innovation they've introduced seeks to answer yes to these two questions, and they're not shy about promoting their record of innovation. As their website proclaims, "We're a company of builders. Of pioneers. It's our job to make bold bets, and we get our energy from inventing on behalf of customers."[1]

Here are just some of the innovations pioneered by Amazon:

- **Redefining what a book is.** In November 2007, Amazon introduced the first digital Kindle with the vision of offering every book, ever written, in any language, all available within sixty seconds. For the first time since Gutenberg invented the printing press in the mid-fifteenth century, there was no need for a book to require paper and ink!
- **Reinventing the traditional fulfillment center.** This is where goods are picked, packed, and shipped. Many of Amazon's seventy fulfillment centers utilize highly sophisticated robotics that speed up the process

and reduce human error. "We like to think of it as a symphony of software, machine learning, computer algorithms, and people," Amazon spokeswoman Kelly Cheeseman told *MIT Technology Review.* "And the people are such an important component; the technology wouldn't mean anything if you didn't have great employees that help interact and engage with it." Very true![2]

- **New product packaging.** For decades, consumer products have been packaged in much the same way, and often in those ubiquitous "clamshell" clear plastic containers. Amazon saw this as a customer pain point. Their response has been "Frustration-Free Packaging," designed with the customer in mind, making it easier to liberate products from their packages while also reducing waste. The innovation started in 2008 by targeting just nineteen of the most annoying clamshell-packed products. Since then, Frustration-Free Packaging has grown to include more than 750,000 products, and the company reports that customers no longer have "wrap rage." As of December 2017, Amazon's sustainable packaging innovations have eliminated 215,000 tons of packaging material and avoided 360 million shipping boxes.[3]

- **Fast, free shipping.** In February 2005, Amazon launched Amazon Prime, the express-shipping membership program covering about a million products. It was a big gamble: in its first year, the company lost many millions of dollars in shipping revenue. But their analysis told them that if they achieved scale, they would be able to significantly lower the cost of fast shipping. Today it's much more than free two-day shipping. Tens of millions of Prime members (Amazon won't give an exact number) enjoy fast, free unlimited shipping on more than thirty million items; unlimited streaming of tens of thousands of movies, TV episodes, and popular music; free photo storage in Amazon Cloud Drive with Amazon Photos; and one free pre-released book a month with Kindle First.

- **Sustainable energy.** Amazon's newest buildings in Seattle will be heated through recycled heat—an innovation made possible by a "district energy" system that works by capturing heat generated at a neighboring non-Amazon data center and recycling that heat through underground water pipes instead of venting it into the atmosphere.

Amazon was the largest corporate purchaser of renewable energy in 2016, with wind and solar farms that will produce 3.6 million megawatts of power annually.

- **Cloud-based IT services.** To track its half a billion products for sale (and that's just the main US website), Amazon needs huge databases, which it builds to be bigger than necessary. Amazon Web Services turned the company's excess and underutilized computing resources into a source of income. For businesses paying for the service, AWS opened the door to scalable, on-demand, metered services. The service turned information technology from a *capital expense* to an *operational expense*. Not only did this have a profound impact on cash flow, it also changed everything from expense management to tax structure because capital expenses must be amortized over years, where operations can be deducted in the year incurred.

- **Inventions.** As of this writing, according to Justia.com, Amazon holds 7,406 patents for new inventions. (Remember, Amazon is supposed to be a retailer of consumer goods, not a Silicon Valley high-tech company!) For example, on March 13, 2018, the company was granted a patent for an "airlift package protection airbag," designed to protect a package (one item or a number of items) that is dropped from within a predetermined height range by an unmanned aerial vehicle (UAV). This means the Amazon drone will be able to drop your item on your patio without having to land, which uses too much energy.[4]

There are many more areas in which Amazon, in its quest to deliver what you want and when you want it, has built a culture of sustained commitment to innovation. Many of these innovations are invisible to you, the consumer. You never see them, but you see their effect, which is what really matters.

THE SIX COMMITMENTS

No, it's not the name of a gospel singing group. The Six Commitments represent the range of investments you and your company need to make to build a strong and durable culture of innovation:

the **6 commitments**

1. time
2. finances
3. acumen
4. spirit
5. resources
6. imagination

1. Time

The most common justification offered by leaders who aren't pursuing an Innovation Mandate is this: "We'd love to innovate, but we just don't have the time. We work full days around here, and it's all we can do to keep up! Nobody has a spare minute to engage in frivolous experiments."

This type of thinking is very shortsighted.

Why? Because the time you and your people spend on innovation—in whatever form it takes—represents an *investment in your future*.

Think of it this way. If your roof were leaking, and you knew it was nearing the end of its service life, would you ignore it or make the investment to replace it? Of course you'd make the investment. It would be a no-brainer.

Likewise, if the current ideas and processes on which your business were based were nearing the end of their usefulness, would you ignore the warning signs or make the investment in new ideas and processes?

Some leaders say, "We don't need new ideas. We run our business on rock-solid, time-honored values that never go out of date!"

We can all agree with the second sentence, and be glad they hold fast to basic values including honesty, hard work, and fair play. But the *tools* they use will go out of date, just like the tools that Amazon once used went out of date and had to be upgraded.

Your supply chain, your marketing, your human resources policies, your IT structure—all are just tools that eventually wear out and need to be superseded by new ones.

At least that's how it works among your competitors. It should work the same way in your business. You do replace worn-out tools with new ones, don't you?

And, as Aaron Martin, senior vice president of strategy and innovation at Providence Health & Services, said, "If you disrupt your own business through innovation, you have a say in the future. If you don't, you're basically leaving it to others to dictate the terms of how the future will go."[5]

In many companies, the necessity for renewal and the development of new ideas is so important that they set aside actual mandated time for innovation.

In 1948, 3M launched its 15 percent program, where 15 percent of employees' time was dedicated to innovation. The Post-it Note was invented during 15 percent time. Organizations such as Google and Hewlett-Packard have both replicated this approach. Gmail, Google Earth, and AdSense were conceived during Google's 20 percent time, which the internet giant has since redefined to be more of a general concept than a hard-and-fast expectation of time spent.

At Kayak, the online travel site, executives set aside a week for the pursuit of the innovative. Primarily to develop team building, Kayak's hack week has produced new ideas that benefit customers, including direct booking, which allows travelers to conduct all their travel business—flights, hotels, and cars—without leaving the website.[6]

With products like Jira, Confluence, Bitbucket, and Hipchat, collaboration software provider Atlassian helps all sorts of teams plan, code, and track projects. During a quarterly event called ShipIt, Atlassian employees have twenty-four hours to build a solution for a product, the company, or the greater world. Then they create three-minute lightning talks to present their projects to the entire company.[7]

Professional networking site LinkedIn launched "[in]cubator," a program that allows any company employee with an idea to organize a team and pitch their project to executive staff once a quarter. [in]cubator is a more-evolved version of the company's "hackdays," in which employees worked on various creative projects one Friday a month. "We see [in]cubator projects as small investments that have the potential to become big wins for the company," wrote the company on its official blog.[8]

Time is a precious commodity. You can use it to just "tread water" and stay afloat, or with a little bit of planning you can invest your time in new ideas that will pay off in the future.

2. Finances

The number two excuse offered by busy executives is, "We don't have the spare cash to put into a fancy innovation program."

But remember this: in your company, *right now*, the sparks of innovation are flashing again and again! People are naturally curious and seek to improve their work. At the very minimum, you need to establish your Innovation Mandate, *capture* these sparks, and *develop* them. Don't stamp them out! They don't always cost money—and they very often *save* money.

Of course, the most robust cultures of innovation include a financial commitment at some level. Some corporations make *huge* investments in innovation. In 2015, PricewaterhouseCoopers conducted a global survey of corporate innovation spending, and compiled a list of the top innovation investors. German auto manufacturer Volkswagen appeared in first place, spending a whopping $15.3 billion on research projects, which equaled almost 6 percent of the company's annual revenue of $269.1 billion. Volkswagen says its spending results from being a "highly competitive and innovative car manufacturer which must fulfill a whole host of environmental and safety standards." Much of that spending has gone into hybrid vehicles and adding new technology, including semi-autonomous features to some of its twelve brands.

Other big spenders in R&D included Samsung ($14.1 billion), Intel ($11.5 billion), Microsoft ($11.4 billion), Roche, Google, Amazon, Toyota, Novartis, and Johnson & Johnson.[9]

As *Fortune* magazine reported, Samsung breaks R&D investment into three business areas, each with their own time horizon:

1. Business unit development teams have a one- to two-year development outlook.

2. Research institutes have a three- to five-year development outlook.

3. The Samsung Advanced Institute of Technology works on projects with a further line of sight.[10]

AstraZeneca, a British-Swedish multinational pharmaceutical and bio-pharmaceutical company, pumped 21.5 percent of its annual revenue into R&D

in 2015—the highest proportion of designated ("ring-fenced") investment of any of the top twenty.

At Google, the company employs about 18,600 people in research and development, and most of its R&D costs go into staffing and personnel support. According to Google's annual report, "Our product development philosophy is to launch innovative products early and often, and then iterate rapidly to make those products even better."[11]

Let's be honest: most business leaders aren't heading up a company the size of Volkswagen or Google. They don't have that kind of budget for *anything*, much less innovation.

That's okay.

It's not *how much* you spend to support innovation in your organization, it's *how* you spend it that counts.

PwC's 2017 "Innovation Benchmark Report," which surveyed executives in more than 1,200 companies, found that nearly all the participating companies believed their innovation efforts had at least a moderately positive impact on both top-line and bottom-line revenue growth, and roughly half the companies reported their investment had a "great" impact on driving their growth, with an equally significant impact on cost management. These findings showed little correlation to the *dollar amount* of the commitment. In fact, PwC reported, "Over the past dozen years, our annual Global Innovation 1000 study has found no statistical relationship between dollars spent on innovation and financial performance, suggesting that the way you spend your innovation dollars is more important than how many of those dollars you spend."[12]

That's right. While investment in innovation is critical, merely throwing money at the problem is not the solution. It's like anything else in life: you can spend your money recklessly and get fleeced, or you can make smart investments and reap the rewards.

Stuart Blyth, CEO at Rubix Digital Solutions, told *Brainstorm* magazine, "Investing in innovation is not a line item on a company's budget, it's an investment of effort and money into the mindset and culture of the company. The change needs to be driven from the top, with chosen champions within the organization to help with change."[13]

3. Acumen

We live in a time of accelerating change where innovation is becoming the norm—or at least it is among your competitors, and hopefully in your company too.

Change means new things enter your world and impact your business—new technologies, processes, customer expectations, external threats.

To master new challenges requires lifelong learning, which leads to acumen: the ability to make good judgments and quick decisions.

In any organization, there can be no Innovation Mandate without continuous learning. This means both being passively open to new ideas and actively seeking to acquire new knowledge.

Your company's openness to receiving new ideas is a product of the leadership you provide from the top and the example you set. That's a good first step.

The next step is to be proactive.

Your company's *active commitment* to learning requires a *deliberate allocation of resources* and the growth of a culture that sanctions and encourages intellectual advancement.

INVEST IN LEARNING

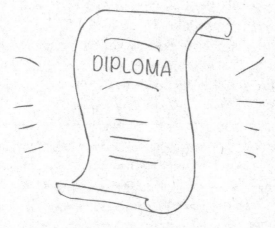

An increasing number of companies subsidize and encourage their employees to pursue formal education.

Health Care Service Corporation (HCSC) is the largest member-owned health insurance company in the United States. Management at HCSC encourages employees of all levels to innovate, contribute ideas, and learn. To back up this commitment, the company offers a variety of programs for team members who want to continue their education. "We provide school reimbursement for undergraduate, master's degrees, and certifications," said Lisa DeWard, senior portfolio delivery consultant, "all while encouraging employees to attend seminars and conferences." As the company says, "We are committed to discovering new ideas, finding a better way, and asking the right questions. Ongoing learning and development opportunities help foster this kind of creative thought."[14]

Smaller companies do it too. As reported by *Fortune*, TD Industries, a construction and real estate company based in Dallas, Texas, spent $1,020,150 on tuition and training reimbursements in 2015, with 92 percent of its 2,300 employees taking advantage of the benefit. Because it's a construction company, more of its employees enroll in classes for technical training—often at night—versus courses for college credit. It considers any cost associated with a class as "tuition."[15]

The website of the company says, "At TD Industries we support a culture of inclusion, a culture of ownership. We accomplish this through a Servant Leadership philosophy that puts others first."[16]

For this and many other aspects of its innovative company culture, it's no surprise that TD Industries has been listed among so many ranks, including:

- 2018 *Fortune* 100 Best Companies to Work For (ranked 73)
- 2017 *People* Companies That Care (ranked 11)
- 2017 Best Workplaces in Texas (ranked 12)
- 2017 *Fortune* 100 Best Companies to Work For (ranked 44)
- 2016 Best Workplaces for Latinos (ranked 9)
- 2016 Best Workplaces to Retire From (ranked 5)

A recent survey by EdAssist, a company that advises employers on their tuition assistance programs, revealed that if asked to choose between similar jobs, nearly 60 percent of respondents would choose the job with a professional development program over one with regular pay raises.[17]

There are many ways you can actively support lifelong learning in your company. By doing so, you'll keep the spark of innovation burning bright in every corner of your organization while making the smart business decisions that bring in profits.

4. Spirit

To create and sustain a culture where the spark of innovation flourishes, we've seen that you need to allocate time, provide financial support, and make the appropriate intellectual commitment.

You also need to have the right *spirit*.

This means you need a culture in which work is fun and the unknown is exciting.

You do not want a culture in which work is drudgery and the unknown is scary.

Employees of the file-sharing service Dropbox benefit from a collaborative environment with plenty of opportunities to grow. A favorite is Hack Week, which allows everyone to return to their roots by tinkering with code or pursuing a professional interest. This freedom makes the problem-solving process seem less intimidating—and often generates inspired solutions that make the office (and employees!) excel.[18]

CarMax, the largest retailer of used cars in the United States, has always sought to transform how vehicles are bought and sold in America by making the experience transparent and stress free. As chief information officer Shamim Mohammad told *MIT Sloan Management Review*, how product teams are managed is key to keeping the spark of innovation alive. "The one thing that every person on the team must have is curiosity," he said. "We're encouraging these agile product teams to learn, explore, and discover how to best deliver against business objectives and exceed customer expectations. In this type of environment, it's important to develop a culture that's not afraid of failure and is motivated by constant learning to enhance the next iteration of the product."[19]

The Innovation Mandate *welcomes* failures because you *learn* from them. And it's often okay to not have a clear goal. As Mohammad remarked, "When we started this journey, we didn't have an exact blueprint for how the culture was going to evolve. But like our agile product teams, we are constantly evaluating how our teams can become more effective and make better decisions."

Here are the four keys to creating a spirit of innovation that gets results:

1. **Keep the effort focused.** Too many corporate visions and missions sound the same: "Become the number one provider of blah, blah, blah." These generic, broad-based goals might seem useful, but they do nothing to spark innovation. Perhaps the worst thing a company can do is to proclaim it wants innovation without giving any direction. That's when the focus gets lost and teams waste time and energy. Instead, be crystal clear about how you want to improve the lives of your customers and solve their problem.

2. **Give your people the gift of time.** You can't expect your employees to innovate and come up with new ideas if they're overloaded with everyday tasks. Either build new ideas into the fabric of everyday work—such as allowing employees to brainstorm as a regular part of a project—or give them chunks of time where they're free to try new ideas.

3. **Applaud failure.** As the American author and pastor John C. Maxwell said, "The difference between average people and achieving people is their perception of and response to failure."[20] As a leader, how do you respond to failure? Do you say, "That's terrible," or do you say, "Good try! What have we learned? What's the next step?" Remember, we're talking not about plain old stupidity, but about an honest failure made while striving to solve a problem. (See point #1 above.)

4. **Recognize success.** Team members need to know that their successes are appreciated and could make a difference. There's no faster way to kill the spirit of innovation than to take an employee's idea or suggestion and then fail to say "thank you."

   Studies have shown that monetary rewards are not the best way to encourage innovation. It's not healthy when the motivation to innovate is the desire for a cash prize.

   In their report "The Dirty Laundry of Employee Award Programs: Evidence from the Field," researchers Timothy Gubler, Ian Larkin, and Lamar Pierce found that reward systems can often backfire. As Larkin told the Harvard Business School newsletter, "When I talk to companies about award programs, I find myself telling them, 'Don't put in that $500 or the trip to the Bahamas.' It sounds like a nice thing to put in, but it also changes the psychological mindset people have."

   It's more effective to make an emotional, human connection with the person you want to recognize. Publicly thank them in front of their peers. "You can't put a price on that," said Larkin. "The recognition of hearing you did a good job and that others are hearing about it is worth more than money."[21]

5. Resources

It's one thing to *say* you support and value innovation.

To make it meaningful, you need to provide the resources to make it possible. You can't make a return if there's no investment of resources. This is true of every business venture, including innovation.

We've talked about two important resources: money and time.

There are others that are just as important.

One of the most important resources is the physical stuff you need to create something new. Every company has equipment it uses—computers, tools, product demos, scraps of failed projects. This equipment is likely being used on a daily basis for core business purposes. In organizations that discourage innovation, the everyday gear is "hands off" unless used for a current business activity. If an employee is trying something new, they are often discouraged from using workplace equipment or may not have access to it at all. In contrast, at organizations committed to innovation at every level, leaders ensure that employees feel comfortable using company equipment to try new ideas.

It's often said that a designated "innovation lab" or room can be counterproductive, because leaders too often set up such a space and then let it wither on the vine. An innovation lab can be the kind of "feel good" project that looks pleasing on the annual report but produces nothing. Recent years have seen Nordstrom, Microsoft, Disney, Target, Coca-Cola, British Airways, and The New York Times Company either close or dramatically downsize their innovation labs. Analysts say that 90 percent of innovation labs are failing.[22]

But if such a space is created with a serious intent, funded and equipped, and actually used by its employees, then an innovation lab can be a good thing. A rare innovation lab success story is Daimler's Lab1886, established in 2007 as Daimler Business Innovation. It works because the company imposes defined milestones, and transparent processes structure the work in the incubator. If an idea does not stand the defined stress test—for example, if the project isn't scalable or won't help the company fulfill its mission—it is discarded. As Daimler said on its website, "Innovation is not by chance. Innovation follows a plan. Driven by the passion to make the unimaginable possible, people experiment with the known and put it together in new ways. To this end, Lab1886 has its own philosophy divided into three consecutive phases: ideation, incubation, commercialization."[23]

6. Imagination

Imagination is the realm of the mind where you see things that do not yet exist in this world, but which one day might.

It's the critical *first step* in innovation.

It's a particularly human trait that allows us to see a problem, project the image into the future, and see the solution. It allows us to take seemingly unrelated ideas and discover how they fit together in unexpected ways. With imagination, we can ask, "What if?" and then visualize a solution.

What if we took ordinary mobile phones and created a money transfer system that anyone could use?

What if we used satellites to provide precise global positioning services for virtually any object on Earth?

What if we leveraged the power of the internet to let people work at home rather than coming to a central office?

What if we got rid of clunky bolt-on solar roof panels and made the entire roof of a house a solar panel?

You'll note that in each of these examples—and countless more—the innovative process requires seeing a problem (such as, billions of people in developing nations don't have access to banks) and then imagining a solution (most of these same bankless people have mobile phones). With the solution having been imagined (somehow we need to connect mobile phones to a money transfer system), all that remains is to figure out how to make it real. In the case of mobile money transfers, in simple terms you "top up" your mobile phone account with credit and then, via text message, transfer it to someone else's account. It seems so simple now that it's real!

Imagination works on a big scale. It isn't particularly relevant in incremental changes. Typical verbal challenge statements like, "What other colors should we offer in our line of sneakers?" or "How might we improve communications across divisions of our global company?" do not inspire the imagination. In fact, they tend to box it in. You get colleagues and others to use their imaginations by stimulating them while eliminating preconceptions. You can even simply *ask* them to imagine. For example, instead of asking, "How can we improve the delivery of our product to our customers?" ask, "Imagine our product arrived at the customer's door exactly on time, every time, regardless of the weather or the day of the week. What would such a delivery system look like? Describe it, or sketch it out." Now you're giving the person a blank canvas free of preconceptions. The imagined solution may be impractical, or it may be a fresh new idea that could disrupt the marketplace.

IMAGINATION GOES BEYOND DATA TO DISRUPTIVE INNOVATION

Businesses like to depend on data to tell them what customers want. Intuition is universally decried. This is legitimate—up to a point. Data is useful on a limited scale, but it can only tell you so much.

How many products have flopped despite reams of market research? How many political elections have defied the data, with the underdog coming out the winner? Many! At the end of the day, customers make decisions based on emotion, not data. They buy what they like, even if they have never seen it before.

Customers often don't consciously know what their real problems are. They know where the immediate pain is, but this is often just a symptom of the real, much deeper concern. It takes time, patience, and imagination to uncover what really motivates them.

Getting to the heart of a customer issue means looking at all the data and then going one step beyond to experience what that problem is like for them—touching, smelling, and tasting what their environment is like and how they operate within it.

In our era, Steve Jobs was the master of imagining what the customer wanted even if the customer wasn't consciously aware of it or could articulate it. As he said, "It's really hard to design products by focus groups. A lot of times, people don't know what they want until you show it to them."[24]

As Mario D'Amico, senior VP of marketing at Cirque du Soleil, wrote in a 2012 theoretical case study published in the *Harvard Business Review*, "How can people tell you what they want if they haven't seen it before? If we ask them what they want, we'll end up doing *Swan Lake* every year!"[25]

If you want to make incremental improvements to an existing product, then by all means use customer surveys and data.

If you want to be disruptive and innovate on a grand scale, forget the data and use your imagination!

A sustained and serious commitment to Time + Financing + Learning + Spirit + Resources + Imagination = Innovation. If you and your organization can make a commitment to each of these foundations of innovation and stick to them for the long term, you'll stay ahead of the innovation curve.

NEED TO BETA TEST AN APP?
GET THE TESTERS DRUNK!

Recently the *New Yorker* profiled Appcues, a Boston-based startup that tests apps to determine how easily people can use them. In a true spark of innovation, the company realized that if you were going to test apps on the target demographic—urbanites age twenty to forty—then you should do it under real-life battle conditions, when the user is harried, or confused, or . . . drunk! Jonathan Kim, the company's twenty-nine-year-old CEO, said, "We asked ourselves, 'How cool would it be to throw a party and let people test apps?'"

The company had done a few drunk app tests in its hometown of Boston. "This usability testing," said the company's website, "will help product teams evaluate their software by watching actual users interact with it. In this setting, attendees will interact with beta versions of a bunch of different products and talk it through with its creators."

On a March evening in 2018, the company rented a space in San Francisco for a West Coast Drunk User Testing. Two hundred and eighty people showed up, presumably by Uber or trolley car. They were mostly male tech workers, and each paid six bucks for the pleasure of drinking all the beer and wine they wanted while testing various apps.

"The idea of intoxicating a large group of people is good to get a lot of data that you might not get otherwise," a software engineer named Amy Loftus told *New Yorker* writer Blaise Zerega.[26]

Innovation takes many forms—including finding new ways to beta test a product!

TAKE ACTION!

To ensure a strong Innovation Mandate, make these Six Commitments:

1. **Time.**

   Your employees need the time to experiment and brainstorm new solutions. Whether it's on a fixed schedule or built into the day, consider their time spent innovating as an investment in your organization's future.

2. **Finances.**

   To start and stay consistent, earmark a line in your budget for the support of innovation. Keep it there even during lean times, because that's when you need it most.

3. **Acumen.**

   Your employees need to be the best and the brightest. Promote and facilitate lifelong learning, make sound business decisions, and the return on investment will be significant.

4. **Spirit.**

   The companies with the lowest rate of employee turnover also have the highest employee-engagement rates and are seen as being happy places to work. People who are unhappy or bored are not innovative. Keep spirits high by making the emotional connections everyone wants yet can't always find.

5. **Resources.**

As the leader, you need to provide the time, the money, and the resources to create a sustainable culture of innovation. Resources include the physical space and the necessary equipment.

6. **Imagination.**

Many conventional problems are solved by asking, "Could we make this existing process incrementally better?" There's nothing wrong with that! But for real innovation, it works better to imagine a perfect world, and then ask, "How would we create our solution? What would it look like?"

Get started today!

6

THE WHOLE ENCHILADA

Would you buy a car that didn't have any wheels?

A phone that didn't have a keypad?

An enchilada that didn't have any cheese?

Of course not.

You want the entire car, the complete phone, and the whole enchilada.

The Innovation Mandate is no different.

If you're going to make the investment in innovation—which you absolutely must do—then you don't want to waste your time, money, and resources on a half-baked, incomplete scheme. You want a robust, holistic program that touches every aspect of your organization. That's how you'll realize the full rewards and the most benefits.

START WITH THE DEFINITION

In order to avoid a half-hearted Innovation Mandate, it's absolutely critical that you first define what it is. That's not exactly profound, yet this simple premise seems to elude many. As the first step toward being complete and holistic, let's talk about what's required.

As you'll recall from earlier in the book, we define innovation as:

> The creation of new value that serves your organization's mission and customer.

The spark of innovation can come from anywhere—a planned innovation lab, a suggestion by an employee, a partnership with another company in a different industry. Each and every spark must be identified and evaluated, and if shown to be promising, then nurtured with the appropriate resources before being subsumed into the everyday operations of the organization.

Doing this successfully, over and over again, requires a holistic approach in which no new idea is allowed to fall through the cracks just because the organization and the people within it weren't capable of exploiting it.

If your innovation lab comes up with a new idea—which, after all, is the point of having an innovation lab in the first place—the organization needs to be prepared to reap its benefits.

If a frontline worker has an idea about how a process could be done better, then that little spark needs to be seen and captured.

If a manager says, "Let's partner with ABC Company to cross-sell to each other's customers," that innovation needs to be assessed and, if deemed worthy, supported to completion.

This is how you stay one step ahead of the competition.

This is how you give your customers what they really crave.

This is how you earn bigger profits.

DEAR DOCTOR:
THE INNOVATION DIAGNOSTIC

If you're not feeling well, you go to your doctor.

You say, "I have a headache," or "my stomach hurts," or whatever is bothering you.

What does your doctor do in response? Choose the correct answer:

A. Admits you to the hospital, takes you into surgery, does the surgery, hopes you recover.

B. Carefully examines you, talks to you about your concern, takes your medical history, and if necessary orders the appropriate tests to identify the problem. Only then will he or she propose a course of treatment.

Obviously the answer is "B." The first step toward better health is always a careful and well-informed diagnosis.

The importance of reaching the correct diagnosis is impressed on every medical student and trainee from the first day of medical school. Why? Because the patient has so much to lose when there is a misdiagnosis. Where a carefully crafted treatment could have returned a patient to full health, the consequences of a wrong diagnosis can be devastating.

Your business is no different.

As you formulate your organizational transformation to become an innovation leader, the first place to start is with a diagnostic. You have to know your current reality before planning how to change it. Then you can roll out your innovation strategy and put it into action.

THE COMMITMENT:
YOU'VE ALREADY GOT THIS, RIGHT?

In the previous chapter we agreed that you shouldn't begin your Innovation Mandate until you have an absolute commitment from the highest levels. There was a comprehensive list of things required to demonstrate a true leadership commitment to innovation. In the sequence of innovation, this is where we must start, and we must not go any further until we feel that the commitment is genuine and complete.

The commitment from the top must include:

- √ Active leadership
- √ Adequate funding
- √ Organizational resources
- √ Education when necessary
- √ Realistic goals
- √ Metrics for measurement
- √ Accountability

Do what Santa does and "check your list twice"!

Just as your doctor will never prescribe treatment without first making an accurate diagnosis, in my practice, we will not even work with an organization until they've agreed to allow us to conduct an *innovation readiness assessment*.

As you build your innovation initiative, your diagnostic needs to include your people, investment, infrastructure, and policies.

PREPARE YOUR PEOPLE FOR PROGRESS

Your people are the heart and soul of your organization. Here are some of the human resource areas you need to diagnose as you plan the organization's transformation to become an innovation leader:

Team architecture. Every organization needs an innovation officer who's responsible for ensuring the organization's innovation transformation is robust and sustained. In a small company, this could be the owner or CEO. But the buck doesn't stop with only one person! The emerging culture of innovation must be infused into every position and person in the company, from the boardroom to the mailroom, and including outside stakeholders.

Cultural appetite for risk. Innovation means failure as well as success. No human being can possibly foresee all the consequences of an innovation, no matter how obvious such consequences may seem in hindsight.

Recent research from Accenture shows that highly innovative companies are essentially no more likely to embrace risk than their less innovative peers, which at first may seem surprising. But when researchers investigated further, they found that highly innovative companies approach the *management of innovation* risk differently, and that their business models are critical factors in their success.[1]

Leading innovators recognize that, far from stifling innovation, sophisticated, state-of-the-art risk management tools and techniques, including small-scale experimentation and portfolio management, can actually help encourage it. They know that by combining a thoughtful risk management approach with innovation, they can create a powerful, value-driving partnership.

Stakeholder incentives. What do stakeholders have to gain—or lose—from a culture of innovation? It's possible that some stakeholders will be left behind, such as factory workers who are laid off when an assembly line becomes automated. Others may benefit, such as a social media platform that reaps a bigger share of advertising dollars because of marketing innovations. Be sure to assess the impact innovations may have on all of your stakeholders.

Internal communications. It's become an axiom in business that noncommunicative silos are bad and barrier-free internal communication is good. This is even more important in a culture of innovation, where change is happening at a faster rate and new paradigms are being introduced.

Good communications can also *spur* innovation because people get better ideas when they network with those outside their own area of expertise. For example, when a product team talks to people from support, sales, and marketing, they will get useful insights that will shed light on what customers want.

Innovation training. Innovating is a skill that can be learned like any other. The most successful innovation training programs are "hands-on," involving participants forming teams, generating real ideas for innovation projects, pitching to their senior leaders, gathering feedback, and refining.

Give basic training to everyone, and then narrow it down. Give more advanced training and then refine again. Eventually, put the biggest investments into individuals who prove innovation capability. In this way you are filtering out costs and risks along the way. But remember—no one is ever completely cut from the innovation club. New ideas can come from anywhere.

If an employee is absolutely incapable of offering a new idea, perhaps they should find employment elsewhere.

Innovation events. While gimmicky "shiny objects" don't work, sometimes a special focus on innovation can be positive. An innovation event is typically a one-day event in which employees form small teams to try and solve a problem relevant to the business. At the end of the day, the teams present their ideas to leaders with a strong business case and working prototype.

For example, as reported by Thoughtworks.com, an innovation day at a bank inspired a solution for the problem of roommates each paying their share of monthly or shared bills, such as for rent or utilities. This new group bill-paying feature was folded into the existing banking app and allowed users to share bills and send texts to their friends telling how much they owe, their bank details, and providing them with a unique reference number that could later be used to track when a friend has paid them.[2]

Why did the bank like the idea? Because the concept was seen as something that no other bank offered and would allow the bank to better serve members of a younger demographic who, from the research, shared bills on a frequent basis.

THE MONEY ANGLE

Organizations are increasingly asking themselves these two questions:

1. How much is our organization investing in innovation?
2. How much do we think we should be investing?

This seems basic, but often leaders just don't know the precise answer or haven't thought in these simple terms.

Harvard Business Review asked a group of managers how innovation dollars should be allocated. Their answers were:

- 75 percent on day-to-day operations
- 5 percent on incremental improvements
- 10 percent on sustaining innovations
- 10 percent on big, disruptive innovations

However, most of the surveyed companies weren't investing at this level. The exercise revealed that organizations instinctively feel they should be spending more on innovation—but many haven't yet made it. Because the vast majority of funds are spent on everyday operations ("keeping the lights on"), the organizational transformation to become an innovation leader often requires being disciplined about segregating funds for improvement and innovation. Without clear allocation toward innovation, the turbulence of day-to-day operations will gobble up the lion's share of resources.[3]

THE NUTS AND BOLTS

In addition to your people, your organization also consists of physical things: buildings, offices, computers, networks, vehicles. All of them can play a part in the organizational transformation to become an innovation leader.

Technology infrastructure. While ideas come from the human mind, in many circumstances you need the technology to make it happen. It can be sophisticated or simple! In the early days of Toyota's adoption of *kaizen*, the assembly line workers communicated with each other by using *kanban* cards (literally "signboard" or "billboard" in Japanese). These were actual colored cards that told downstream workers if, for example, there was a parts shortage. Many project managers still use *kanban* cards today on a *kanban* board serving as their team's central information hub.

At the other end of the spectrum, many companies are using sophisticated innovation software programs that allow team members and leaders to capture, manage, and vote on ideas that eventually lead to the best innovations. High-end, process-driven, and outcome-focused tools offer innovation workflows that support innovation management, end-to-end. While being highly strategic and making idea development integral, they are also focused on analytics, execution, portfolio management, piloting, and trends.

THE PAPERWORK

What business would be complete without a big fat *Policies & Procedures Manual*? Hopefully yours is very brief and concise! While innovation should be fun, it also needs guidance and a set of rules that everyone agrees on:

Specific goals. Top innovating companies approach innovation the same way they approach any other business metric: they want measured success.

For example, one metric used by many companies is the "innovation sales rate" (ISR), which is usually defined as a measure of the percentage of sales made by sales of new products.

Another key measure of innovation and creativity is how many ideas per month your company is getting from all of your employees. According to analysts, the average Japanese company receives one hundred times more written ideas than the average American company. As American manufacturing rebounds from decades of decline, that metric is changing. You can see it clearly in companies like General Motors, where in the past decade the culture has changed dramatically for the better.

Many companies measure the risk-adjusted net present value of the innovation pipeline and the return on investment in that pipeline.

Policies, procedures, and systems. You might think that having too many policies and procedures will stifle the spark of innovation, not promote it. In many cases, this is true. If you make the process of offering new ideas cumbersome or difficult to navigate, you'll kill it.

What we're talking about are policies designed to *encourage* and *exploit* innovation. Establishing policies promoting innovation means setting clear priorities and goals, defining an organized approach to accomplishing the work, and allocating resources effectively and properly.

Organizations with a robust Innovation Mandate put systems in place such as integrated customer touchpoint management, where the voice of customers is ably captured, categorized, and then funneled to whatever department needs customer feedback. Perhaps most importantly, programs must be created to reward innovative efforts that include public recognition, sending a clear message that innovation is valued.

Formal Innovation Mandate strategy. An emerging innovation culture can be created and supported through planned activities such as idea challenges, venture-capital style incubation funds, and catalyst teams, all of which increase the number and quality of transformational ideas. Companies that successfully manage innovation as an evolving competency can improve operational effectiveness, increase revenue, and pursue new business models or business structures.

Managing innovation requires new ways of thinking and working. It begins by drafting a charter to gain agreement on the vision for the initiative while staying in alignment with business goals. Scope the initiative, and establish the budget and resources.

Intellectual property policies. Since innovations are by definition new ideas and are often new inventions, it's important that all team members understand the laws governing what is a work for hire—that is, work produced while on the company payroll and using company resources is owned by the company.

Critical to an employer's ownership of intellectual property is a written agreement with the employee that specifically assigns to the company any and all intellectual property created by the employee during the course of their employment with the company. Such an agreement is often called an "assignment of inventions" or "ownership of discoveries" agreement.

Innovation report outs. Everyone hates writing reports . . . but these have value because everyone can learn from them. An innovation evaluation report has a number of purposes:

- A clear judgment of the success or failure of your project, primarily aimed at other practitioners (usually via the executive summary). Remember that in an organization dedicated to sustained innovation, failures will be just as common as successes, and they'll carry many valuable lessons.
- More detail on the project, so that others can follow in your footsteps or understand the project in detail and either replicate it or try it some other way.
- Clarity on the implications and limitations of your evaluation so that others can understand the overall context of your research.

If you want a prefab outline, you can download prepared project progress report templates.

This is just a small sampling of the kinds of things you need to look at to determine your organization's current state of readiness. Although it is true that innovation should have some fluidity, it also has to have a life support system that's based on evidentiary support of what works and what does not work.

The question to you is . . . Are you ready?

THE PLAN
OF ATTACK

Once your doctor has worked up a robust diagnosis of your problem, then he or she will write up a treatment plan.

The same holds true for your company and your organizational transformation to become an innovation leader. As the old cliché suggests, "Failing to plan is planning to fail." How true!

Like all organizational disciplines, innovation requires a plan that will allow you to avoid many costly potential problems when compared to doing it on the fly. Your innovation operating system will give you the infrastructure you need to ensure that you avoid the common pitfalls while significantly proving the likelihood for meaningful and measurable success.

SPONTANEITY IS GOOD . . .
UP TO A POINT

Sparks of innovation can come unexpectedly from anywhere at any time.

They can also be deliberately engineered.

In both cases, the little fellows need to be captured and carefully introduced into the innovation pipeline.

All too often, hastily planned brainstorming sessions bring up a lot of good ideas that somehow never get used, while the boring kinds of ideas you are trying to get away from seem to be used again and again. One reason for this is the lack of an innovation plan.

In your office, you've probably heard the boss say something like this:

"We need fresh ideas for the XYZ Company proposal! Let's take a meeting and brainstorm ideas."

How often have the creative ideas of the brainstorming session actually been implemented?

Ideas are fine, but unless they're backed up by action, they won't benefit your organization.

An innovation plan gives structure and backbone to spontaneous ideas. A plan provides a set of directions for how to take the fragile spark of innovation and nurture it and help it come to full fruition.

CELEBRATE SUCCESSES
AND LEVERAGE FAILURES

Innovation means seeking new ideas, thinking outside the box, imagining what isn't there, and embracing risk.

It means celebrating successes.

Failures? It means identifying them, quickly killing them, and then learning from them. People who have tried something new and come up short, for whatever reason, need to be recognized and thanked for their effort. And we're not talking about handing out silly "participation" trophies as they do in some elementary schools. That's not helpful. It's about using failure as a springboard to true innovation.

In a holistic innovation culture, managing failures is not always easy, especially in the typical corporate culture that penalizes them. This is where personal leadership is critical. The leader must set the tone and live the values of the innovative organization.

Over and over again throughout history, we see how successes have sprung from failures.

KNOW WHEN TO KILL A BAD IDEA

It's important to nurture and develop good innovations. They are like money in the bank.

It's equally important to decisively kill ideas that aren't going to work.

Don't judge them, don't lay blame, don't engage in recrimination—just get the weeds out of your garden.

When Steve Jobs returned to Apple in 1997 to retake the reins, he famously slashed Apple's product pipeline from 150 products to just four—one desktop and one portable device each for consumers and professionals. He said, "Deciding what not to do is as important as deciding what to do. It's true for companies, and it's true for products."[4]

The move to a smaller product line and a greater focus on quality and innovation paid off. During Jobs's first fiscal year after his return, ending in September 1997, Apple lost $1.04 billion and was "ninety days from being insolvent," as Walter Isaacson wrote in his biography of Jobs. One year later, the company turned a $309 million profit.[5]

In the pages ahead, you'll find the template you need to build out your innovation initiative in a practical way.

The previous chapter and this chapter made two very important points: the biggest sources of innovation success are *commitment* and *completeness*.

Remember that innovation can be a blast! It's what we're here to do, and hopefully this book can help you take advantage of the incredible opportunity to have fun and deliver enterprise value while serving your beloved customer.

SLACK: FROM FAILURE CAME SUCCESS

A few years after selling Flickr in 2005, Stuart Butterfield and his co-founders started a video game company, Tiny Speck, focused on the multiplayer online experience. But their timing was off, and they invested millions into the PC realm when mobile was rising. Realizing their mistake, they closed down Tiny Speck and went back to the drawing board. While they were working on the game, though, they had created an extensive internal chat system that allowed them to quickly communicate and share files with each other. They called it "Searchable Log of All Conversation and Knowledge," or Slack.[6] On a whim, they began sharing this team chat system with friends at Microsoft and other companies. The response was immediate and positive, and Butterfield realized that their simple side project, not their complicated video game, was their real hit.

As of February 2018, the site had grown to nine million daily users and an estimated $200 million in annual revenue.

If their video game hadn't totally failed, the team may never have turned their attention to what would become a huge success. Butterfield and his team were so focused on the big game that they didn't notice the extremely valuable tool they were innovating. With the shadow of the big project removed, they suddenly saw the potential in all the other parts of their work.

1. **Start with an accurate diagnosis of your organization.**

   You can't make a plan unless you know where you're starting from. Be honest. Don't sugarcoat reality. If you have work to do to create a robust Innovation Mandate, then do it.

2. **Ensure you have commitment from the top.**

   I've said it before and it bears repeating: absent a powerful message of support from leadership, your employees will likely assume a default position of risk avoidance. They will play it safe, because no one can blame you if you do what you're told and don't make any mistakes. This is not what you want! Your organization needs a constant sparking of new ideas, and you need to be clear that new ideas are both wanted and expected.

3. **Lay the groundwork for success.**

   Review the key functional areas—your people, finances, the nuts and bolts, and the paperwork. Ensure that they all work together to support innovation. Set metrics for measuring innovation success.

4. **Celebrate success, learn from failures.**

   Don't be coy or secretive. When a new idea works, make sure everyone knows, and identify the people responsible. Avoid monetary rewards, because you don't want that to become the primary motivator.

   When failures happen, identify them quickly and delete them. Let your people know that sincere failures are expected, and that every failure is one step closer to a breakthrough. Keep the focus on always trying to fulfill the mission of your organization.

SYSTEMS = GOOD, CHAOS = BAD

Everyone in business knows the value of systems.

A system is a repeatable process in your business that can theoretically take place without the direct action of a leader or manager. A system is a method of doing something that can be done the same way, over and over, as efficiently as possible. It allows leaders to focus on future growth and moving beyond mere survival to true prosperity.

The alternative to a well-constructed system is chaos. This is the painful condition known to both startups and big corporations, where every day you need to reinvent the wheel. Instead of coaxing the spark of innovation to life, you're running around putting out damaging fires. You can't plan for the future because you're too busy managing the present and its many small crises.

Systems can be simple or complex. A simple example in a small business might be an email autoresponder sequence that nurtures a relationship between you and the people who subscribe to your mailing list. It might be a system that triggers an invoice when a certain part of a project is marked as complete.

The bigger the business, the more systems it will have. Big companies have systems for supply chain, sales, production, hiring, branding, marketing—just about every facet of their operations.

Companies that are built on a franchise model are nothing *but* systems. If you're just counting the number of franchisees, the reigning king of the franchise world is 7-Eleven. With fifty-eight thousand stores operating in seventeen countries worldwide, 7-Eleven has its systems fine-tuned. If you want to open your own 7-Eleven, pretty much all you have to do is plunk down anywhere from $37,550 to $1.2 million (depending on location and other variables), get the 7-Eleven training, and unlock your front door! Services provided by the home office in Dallas, Texas, include obtaining and bearing the ongoing cost of the land, building, and store equipment; record keeping, bill paying, and payroll services for store operations; and fees and financing for all normal store-operating expenses. The head office for 7-Eleven even pays for the franchisee's water, sewer, gas, and electric utilities.[1]

They've got their systems fine-tuned to a science.

But having massive operational systems does not by itself guarantee success. Just ask Blockbuster. At its height in 2004, the video rental franchise giant employed 84,300 people worldwide and had 9,094 stores in total, with more than 4,500 of these in the United States. They ruled the video rental business! But the market vanished, their business systems became obsolete, and in 2010 the company declared bankruptcy.

Some companies—but not nearly enough!—have systems for innovation. But I'll get to that in a moment.

THE BEST SYSTEMS ARE FLEXIBLE

In many ways, systems are amazingly good.

Without systems, people have to solve the same problem over and over again. Systems ensure consistency, promote thrift, and reduce repetitive tasks that don't add value. They guarantee that when you order a Big Mac in Boise, it's the same Big Mac that you'll get in Baton Rouge or Bangor. It also means that McDonald's can scale up production of Big Macs and accurately predict the profit margin regardless of whether the Big Mac is sold in Topeka or Tokyo.

But systems can easily turn nasty. They can change from being a friend of an organization to being its worst enemy.

They can become entrenched and resistant to progress. When external conditions change—as they are in today's business environment with increasing speed and depth—people can cling to established systems in the false belief that what is "tried and true" will save the day.

Russell Ackoff, one of the pioneers of business systems, warned against organizational silos, sclerosis, and fragmentation. Ackoff defined the systems age as beginning after World War II, during a time of growing global and technological complexity. Organizations would henceforth have to deal with "sets of interacting problems," and the key challenge would be designing systems that would *learn and adapt*. He said, "Experience is not the best teacher; it is not even a good teacher. It is too slow, too imprecise, and too ambiguous." Organizations need to learn and adapt through experimentation, which he said "is faster, more precise, and less ambiguous. We have to design systems which are managed experimentally, as opposed to experientially."[2]

The moral of this story is that while systems are mandatory for any thriving business, these systems must be agile. They must bend, not break. They must be capable of being reinvented as conditions change.

For any of these conditions to be met, a system must be as *simple* as possible.

THE USER-FRIENDLY
APPLE OPERATING SYSTEM

Remember those ancient days before everyone had a smartphone or even a home computer?

Back in the Dark Ages of the 1970s, when computers were beginning to be made in sizes smaller than a refrigerator, the biggest obstacle to their use by ordinary people was their complexity. You had to learn to use command-line prompts to drive the operating system. Punch cards ruled, and while desktop calculators did the math, typewriters did the word processing.

Apple made using a computer intuitive. The Mac operating system, with its desktop and bitmapped graphical displays, was far easier to use and required less training and expertise than the ubiquitous DOS systems. The Mac was the first truly popular computer with a graphical user interface, a mouse, and the ability to show you what a printed document would look like before you printed it.

What this meant is that the user could, without any special computer training, easily master the system and be productive. The user didn't have to expend time and energy learning how to perform a task. The best industrial systems are like that—they're as simple and easy to learn as possible.

Innovation must also be *sustained over time*. Again, look at Apple. Today the company makes the one computer in the world that is as easy to use as a toaster—the iPhone. The most revolutionary thing about Apple's first iPhone was the seemingly effortless way in which nearly every bit of complexity was hidden behind a display of easy-to-understand icons. The iPhone contained no visible "directory structure."

Your music was not in a particular place on your phone, requiring you to hunt for it; you accessed it by launching the music player with one touch.

COMPLEX MANAGEMENT SYSTEMS
CAN BE DEADLY

In a successful Innovation Mandate, you'll find simple systems that deliver exceptional enterprise value. This includes not only R&D and production systems but *management systems.*

This seems like an obvious formulation, but all too often organizations get tangled up in complicated and bureaucratic systems that actually *stifle* innovation.

The classic example of bureaucracy stifling innovation—with tragic results—is the General Motors ignition switch scandal of the early part of this century. Eventually, GM had to recall nearly thirty million cars worldwide and the company paid compensation for 124 deaths.

The fault had been known to GM for at least a decade prior to the recall being declared. The problem was unintended ignition switch shut-off because a part called the "switch detent plunger," designed to provide enough mechanical resistance to prevent accidental rotation, was insufficient.

According to an email chain from 2005 unearthed by investigators, GM's managers estimated that replacing the key ignition switch component would cost ninety cents per car but only save ten to fifteen cents on warranty costs. Somewhere deep in the bowels of the vast GM bureaucracy, the fix was repeatedly rejected until 2006—but millions of earlier cars weren't recalled.[3]

Remember—innovation is *not* narrowly defined as "a new invention that no one has ever seen before." That's much too limiting. Innovation includes *identifying problems and fixing them.* It means *making a change to the status quo to add value to the product or service.*

FOUR OBSTACLES TO INNOVATION—AND THE SOLUTIONS

Systems can be beneficial or they can hold you back. They can be written down in company manuals, like the comprehensive systems used by 7-Eleven, or they can reside in the guts of the company culture. The latter variety often takes the form of institutional knowledge, or to put it in familiar terms, "That's the way we do it around here."

If "the way we do it around here" is supportive of innovation, that's good.

If it means being stuck in a rut, that's bad.

A system for innovation must be capable of taking the spark of a new idea and developing it into a source of energy. There are at least four significant reasons why corporate innovation is so difficult—but for every problem there's a solution.

1. Previous Success

Problem: When you sell a product and it does well, you've now set the bar. You've hit goals that you want to exceed in the future. This can create a mentality of "if it ain't broke, don't fix it." The organization learns and codifies what made it successful, which locks in a way of doing business and a set of expectations about current and future success.

Solution: It's understandable that it can be difficult to tinker with a successful product, which is why many leading innovators like 3M aim to generate a set amount of revenues from *new* products. In addition, as we can see with many innovative manufacturers like Toyota and, more recently, just about every other car manufacturer, massive innovations happen in the production *process*, out of sight of the consumer. While Toyotas change very little in their exterior appearance from year to year, improvements are always being made under the hood.

If you have a successful product that people love, you're well advised to carefully preserve your market and your brand appeal. But there are still plenty of ways you should be innovating behind the scenes!

2. Catering to the Existing Customer

Problem: Everyone knows that it costs more to acquire a new customer as opposed to keeping an existing one. You know what existing customers want and it's easy to give it to them.

For an entrepreneur, every consumer is a prospect, and there's no infrastructure or product portfolio to support or defend. But established firms, having achieved sales success and having built a product portfolio, want to lock in their customers.

They're more inclined to defend their existing customer base rather than innovate to offer new solutions to new customers.

Solution: The innovative organization knows that consumer tastes change—often dramatically! Consider the soft drink industry. You'd think that Coca-Cola was a foolproof product with decades of customer loyalty. Nope! Sales of the company's iconic soft drinks have been sagging for over twenty years as consumers seek healthier beverages. Sandy Douglas, the company's top North America executive, told trade publication *Beverage Digest* that Coca-Cola is "moving at the speed of the consumer" in its flagship market by evolving both its business model and how it measures success. Shifts in the consumer landscape have inspired the beverage giant to rethink its core success metrics. "We will measure ourselves on what people are willing to pay for our products, not the gallons they purchase," said Douglas. "If you follow your consumer, you're likely to have a good day."

3. Resource Allocation and Project Prioritization

Problem: In any organization, there's only so much money, time, and resources to go around. Corporate innovators often find themselves fighting for limited funds, since the vast majority of resources and dollars are going to support existing products—the cash cows. In addition, executives often can't decide between innovation projects. This leads to half-hearted initiatives and piecemeal innovation that is either ineffective or doomed to fail.

Solution: This is where leaders need to step up and define the culture of the organization. It's incredibly foolish to expect that your product or service will be the same in five or ten years as it is today. To meet the challenge of inevitable massive change, leaders need to mandate an *investment in innovation* with the understanding that new ideas are the lifeblood of the business and are worth paying for. Leaders need to look ahead and take the necessary steps to not only cope with change but to leverage it.

Some industries, such as pharmaceuticals and entertainment, know their products are destined to lose value over time, and that creating new products—proprietary drugs, movies, popular music—is the only way to survive. They know they must *innovate or die*. It's a liberating feeling!

4. Leaders and Employees Are Stubborn

Problem: People can be rigid and set in their ways! Both leaders and employees can have a fear of failure or simply an aversion to changing how they do their work. They get set in their ways, and view innovation as a painful intrusion into their comfortable routine.

Solution: Do you know what's *really* painful? Going out of business because of a failure to keep pace with the inexorable changes that happen in every marketplace. That's painful for everyone.

To create a strong Innovation Mandate, leaders need to be proactive about connecting with their stakeholders. Employees need to fully understand what innovation means and how it's going to be managed in their organization. When there are gaps in that information, employees get nervous and rumors start to spread. Leaders need to clarify gray areas and make sure misinformation isn't spreading.

Call a team meeting and explain what's going on in a clear and concise manner. If your company is big, train your managers to do it. Imagine you're pitching your idea to potential investors—after all, your employees are being asked to invest their time and even their hopes—and start at the beginning. Discuss why innovation is important, and why you're so excited about it. Employees who are afraid to think innovatively won't. Traditional employee training and development often do not include support for idea generation and encouragement to think differently. If you want your company to be truly innovative, then put in place the environment that allows your top managers to teach innovative thinking to their people. If you want to foster an environment of idea generation, then you need to encourage new and risky ideas to be voiced.

Make your innovation operating system no different from any other system in your organization. Fund it properly, educate your stakeholders, and make it simple. Set attainable goals and celebrate both successes and failures. Bring the spark of innovation to every part of your organization and see the powerful results.

ACT, MAKE, IMPACT: THE INNOVATION ECOSYSTEM

Just like a computer needs a frame for support and a case to enclose it, your innovation operating system will need a broad, overarching structure. A simple framework that gives it shape and makes it easy to conceptualize. Something that's easy to diagram.

It's the innovation ecosystem.

The Elements of Innovation

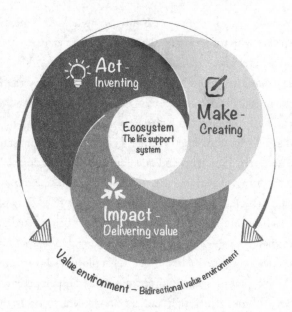

To support sustainable and successful innovation, your organization needs a comprehensive innovation ecosystem. It's the organization's systems, processes, tools, enabling technologies, culture, people, and anything else that provides the life support system for innovation to succeed. Innovative organizations have robust and complete innovation ecosystems, providing the necessary nutrients and culture to drive sustainable enterprise innovation.

You're not likely to act on innovation without the proper ecosystem providing support, and you will not be able to make an impact without the right infrastructure. The ecosystem includes two bidirectional relationships: between external customers and the organization, and between external innovators in the organization in the form of the value environment.

The value environment is not just the marketplace you serve; it's also composed of external innovators and partners with whom you connect in a very bidirectional way. In other words, innovation is very much a two-way street. The best organizations in the world collaborate with external partners, customers, innovators, and even competitors to find new ways to create meaningful enterprise and customer value.

The innovation ecosystem is composed of three equally important phases.

Act

Fed by customer and market insights, business goals, and other external forces, the act of innovation comprises everything related to creating or identifying potential innovations.

It begins with a small spark of an idea that may deliver value to our organization, our mission, and our customer, and then we refine it. Innovation can occur through a wide range of activities that include design thinking, ideation, serendipitous innovation, planned innovation, new product development processes, hackathons, ideation that leverages game mechanics, social innovation, crowdsourcing—the list goes on and on.

Then you determine whether the idea has the potential to hit a target—that is to say, fulfill a need, solve a problem, or create an opportunity. Once you've identified the need, problem, or opportunity, then you can leverage the act of inventing to move you closer to an innovation that delivers real value.

The innovation process should be as complete as possible and should continue to identify ways to add both layered and dynamic value.

Layered value, or value stacking, is the process of adding more value to an idea, ideally without adding additional cost or complexity. Remember that the market is looking for the most value at the lowest cost.

Dynamic value suggests value that actually makes the product, technology, or solution always get better. Your iPhone is probably more valuable today than it was last week. Why? Because Apple has a community of financially engaged external app developers constantly creating a wide range of new apps to make the user's life better at a very low cost, or in many cases at no cost.

The act phase includes the spark generator and fast filter of the innovation pipeline, in which the organization screens ideas to determine if they meet the qualifications of acceptable innovations. For example, an automobile company may have an idea for a great motorcycle, but it may not be a fit given their lack of market expertise and distribution channels. In the innovation pipeline, we start with the directionless spark, and then we move into the assessment and optimization phases.

Make

Make refers to everything related to the creation or implementation of an innovation. It speaks to the process of transmuting ideas into genuine value to the organization and the customers it serves.

In this phase, you will begin the process of taking your design concept and moving it into development. During this phase, you will be gaining insights to verify the business case for your idea. Even if your idea isn't a bright shiny object, you'll need to continue to determine if the innovation serves the intended target.

For example, you may be looking for ways to get clean drinking water to an underserved population in South America. The underserved population is a potential customer base, and you need to be able to distribute and deliver your innovative product. The make phase, as with the active inventing phase, requires that you constantly verify your original value proposition. During the make phase of a new product, you will be optimizing your idea by looking at everything from the best manufacturing methods, materials, packaging, cost of goods sold, financial analysis, surveys, and focus data from customers and everything else that's necessary to make sure there is a business case for your idea.

Your new product innovation has to thrive in an external marketplace with demanding customers and fierce competition. Many viable innovations fail because they were launched to the marketplace before they were done "cooking." Be sure to optimize your innovation before transferring it to the impact phase.

You should also avoid personally evaluating the market viability of your innovation, as you probably won't be able to be objective. During this phase, you may be using traditional new product development methods; some of the most common are referred to as "stage gate," or our preferred method, the opportunity pipeline. The idea of these linear processes is to allow you to go through the evaluation of your idea to verify its business case while concurrently improving the design through dynamic innovation and layering or stacking the innovation.

Impact

Impact is how effectively you take the innovation to the marketplace and create sustainable value. For example, if you've invented a new process to increase efficiency on an assembly line, then you would have to determine how to apply the idea to that process in a way that either enhances the value to the customer or allows you to charge the customer a lower price for your product. The same is true with any product, technology, marketing innovation, or any other type of idea. If it doesn't have a positive impact on your organization or customer, it's not an innovation.

The impact phase is where you create the market life support system for your innovation. This is an important phase, as some of the best innovations are not new inventions but rather innovative business models or delivery mechanisms. For example, Uber did not reinvent the automobile; they created a new ride-for-hire model that connected car owners with customers who were looking for transportation. Likewise, Netflix did not reinvent the internet; they invented a new approach toward delivering content by leveraging digital connectivity.

The goal of any new product innovation is to positively impact the customer. Your marketing strategy, channel strategy, distribution options, engagement strategies, and all the other elements that go into releasing your innovation to the marketplace will be critical to its success. Give your innovation a fighting chance by building out a comprehensive impact plan that addresses all of the aspects of what's necessary to deliver exceptional innovations in a time of market disruption.

In a time of massive market disruption, your innovation needs to be highly differentiated and layered with dynamic value. Before you launch, get real insights about how the market and your customers will perceive your innovation. Optimize your innovation through better channel, distribution, packaging, and other adjunct innovations.

And always be realistic about market projections and customer acceptance!

LESSONS FROM THE WORLD'S BIGGEST NURSING HACKATHON

While at some companies hackathons are nothing more than gimmicks, truly innovative organizations, including Facebook, Hasbro, Unilever, PayPal, the American Nursing Association (ANA), and others, effectively use hackathons as part of a robust innovation operating system. Their hackathons work because the companies are committed to innovation, and they're just one tool in the kit.

The American Nursing Association does an amazing job of serving their members by helping them leverage the skill sets and the insights that will affect the way in which they deliver safe and efficacious care. A great example of their embrace of the spark of innovation was the world's biggest nursing hackathon, held in March 2018 in Orlando, Florida.

In this case, eight hundred participants used innovative thinking to determine ways to advance safe patient handling and mobility, prevent violence against nurses, strengthen moral resilience and ethical practice, and protect health-care workers against needlestick and sharps injuries. Nurses initially generated ideas on their own at group tables, and in a succession of votes, whittled them down to winning solutions.

This ANA hackathon was no small matter, as historically innovation has too often lived only in the corner offices of hospitals and clinics. The ANA recognizes that, every single day, nurses get unfiltered, firsthand knowledge of problems and opportunities. On both a short-term and long-term basis, they work closely with patients. (In other industries, they're called customers.) Because of their frontline experience, practicing nurses have more ideas on how to make things better for the nurse, doctor, patient, and organization than anyone else.

During the hackathon, these amazing nurses unleashed their innate power to innovate, solve problems, and identify new opportunities. "We need to get people to believe in their own creativity," said Karen Tilstra, PhD, co-founder of the Florida Hospital Innovation Lab, where nurses and others can bring their challenges and innovate solutions. "Innovation is always a step in the dark," she added. "It takes courage. But you don't have to know everything to start finding solutions."[4]

As the ANA reported, here are just a few examples of nurses' innovative thinking from the Orlando hackathon:[5]

- A relaxing virtual reality room where nurses can take a break from their unit
- An app in which nurses could report any violent incidents, as well as track the total number of incidents in twenty-four hours
- Gloves that serve as armor against needlesticks and sharps injuries

Are any of these ideas seismic or disruptive? Probably not.

Could these incremental ideas (and others), when accumulated and applied consistently day after day, make a huge difference to an organization's ability to deliver value to its customers and drive up profits?

Absolutely yes!

The hackathon was an amazing example of opening the floodgates of ideas to get new perspectives from the very individuals who have the best actionable insights to drive innovation. We are now seeing this process ramp up as more and more organizations are beginning to see that collaborative organizations that build out simple but powerful innovation pipelines are constantly leading their markets and new innovations in customer satisfaction.

TAKE ACTION!

1. **Start planning your innovation operating system.**

   Your Innovation Mandate begins with the goal of achieving strategic advantage in the marketplace, so in the planning phase you should think specifically about how innovation is going to add value to your strategic intents, and focus on the areas where innovation has the greatest potential to provide strategic advantage. In the well-managed innovation effort, you expect insights to come about as the result of carefully constructed and managed processes and activities, not by random chance.

2. **Keep it simple!**

   Complexity does two things: it discourages the sometimes sensitive human beings, who find they must either play politics or thread their way through a bewildering environment to promote a new idea; and it makes even routine incremental advances much more difficult.

3. **Engage your stakeholders from the top down.**

   Innovation will be driven by the people who work in your organization, and they need to be 100 percent on board. At the end of the day, the Innovation Mandate is all about trust and awareness. Your stakeholders need to trust that their efforts will not go unnoticed and that failure is to be expected, and they need to be aware that innovation needs to be as natural as any other job function.

4. **Position your company for innovation success.**

   Like Coca-Cola, align your organization around the dictates of the market. Empower each team member to make decisions that apply to their own groups and roles. For the highest level of engagement, help your employees align their own self-interest with the organization's interests. Allow your team members to migrate into new groups and to align themselves with their own self-interests within the company. Hire only people who will think outside the box and devise unique solutions to complex problems.

5. **Use the Act, Make, Impact framework.**

   This is the broad supporting structure of your Innovation Mandate. Ensure it's robust, durable, and has the full commitment of the organization.

THE INNOVATION OPERATING SYSTEM (IOS)

We use the term "innovation operating system" for a reason.

Your IOS is very similar to your computer operating system, in that the goal of the system is to *run the machine*. An operating system or OS is a set of programs on the hard drive that enables the computer hardware to communicate and operate with the computer software. It manages the hardware devices in your computer—things like the processor, memory, disk storage, keyboard, mouse, monitor, USB bus, and network adapter. Without a computer operating system, a computer and software program would be useless. A good computer operating system does its work invisibly, efficiently, and profitably. It's durable and requires only regular, anticipated upgrades to stay at peak performance.

Computer operating systems have names like Windows, Linux, Android, and Mac OS.

In addition to running the machine, computer operating systems are augmented by a range of specialized software packages designed to perform specific tasks. These software applications include things like word processing, spreadsheets, presentation software, and the like. Examples include Microsoft Office, Google Chrome, and Adobe Photoshop.

These are all commercial, mass-produced solutions. They are tried and true.

But your company is unique. An off-the-shelf computer software system isn't going to align with what you need. You need solutions that support your individual requirements.

That's why organizations are served by software vendors such as Intellectsoft, MojoTech, DataArt, and FrogSlayer, who custom-craft software systems to meet their needs. The results are hybrid systems that have a basic architecture that's common to all, combined with features that are unique to the customer.

Your innovation operating system will be no different. It will have a basic structure that's similar to others in its class while at the same time having features that are unique to your organization.

We call it *structured customization*. The key to a successful innovation program is that you need to follow a plan that ensures you avoid the common mistakes and pitfalls of enterprise innovation, while at the same time customizing it to fit the unique and special goals, needs, opportunities, and culture of your enterprise.

CREATE YOUR IOS PROGRAMMING CODE IN SIX STEPS

All operating systems are constructed using code. The programming code is basically the rules that apply to the way in which the operating system controls the machine. All code is created using authoring platforms or languages.

Rather than diving too deeply into the analogy and going into all of the complexity of the language, I'm going to describe the building blocks of your IOS code, so that you can create an effective and efficient innovation infrastructure that will deliver real results to your organization.

You'll note that some of these steps dovetail with the work you've already done while formulating your innovation mission. That's fine—some overlap is okay. For example, the first step is to answer the question, "Why?" You may have figured this out and put it into your innovation mission. Good! Then you'll be able to breeze through it to the next step.

Let's get started.

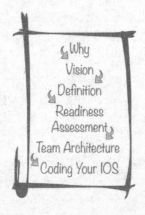

Why
Vision
Definition
Readiness
Assessment
Team Architecture
Coding Your IOS

1. The Why

If you've ever been around children, you probably know the story of the child who, to every answer you give, responds by asking, "Why?"

"I want you to come inside," you say.

"Why?"

"Because it's raining out."

"Why?"

"Because the clouds are full of water, and they can't hold it anymore."

"Why?"

"Because cool air can't hold as much water as warm air."

"Why?"

And so on. You get the idea. If you both keep playing the game, eventually you'll work your way back to the Big Bang theory.

It's funny, but this shows why this question is both *important* and *challenging*.

It's important because it goes to the very heart of how the spark of innovation is vital to your organization. It's challenging because it takes mental effort to answer.

The "why" is critical because it drives stakeholder engagement, establishes measurements for success, and controls the ability to target and navigate through the entire process of innovation. Asking yourself *why* innovation is critical to your organization and what you intend to do with it is truly the genesis of all innovation initiatives.

Perhaps the somewhat slippery and daunting nature of the question is why many executives rush to create an innovation initiative before they have asked themselves why they're doing it in the first place. But this is putting the cart before the horse.

If you're having a difficult time answering the question "Why innovate?" then consider this quote from Edith Widder, American oceanographer, marine biologist, and the co-founder, CEO, and senior scientist at the Ocean Research & Conservation Association: "Exploration is the engine that drives innovation. Innovation drives economic growth."[1]

In her case, she's talking about literal exploration, as in getting in a submarine and going to the deepest part of the ocean to search for giant squids. Your exploration may be physical, like hers, or it may take the form of searching for new ideas, processes, and business solutions.

Just as importantly, Edith Widder stated the second half of the equation: "Innovation drives economic growth." This is so fundamental you can print it on a big banner and hang it on your wall.

Exploring for new ideas drives innovation, which drives economic growth. This is absolutely true for any organization, including yours.

But to get back to how *your* organization answers the question. Too often, "innovation meetings" or "round tables" are empty vessels, but if you're sincere about it, then hosting an open discussion with stakeholders is a good way to start. Get people talking about it. Make innovation an ordinary topic of discussion on the same level as a sales report or new product rollout project. Remove the mystery and unfamiliarity. Make innovation part of the everyday fabric of your organization.

By the way, you don't need just one "why." In fact, you may have several. Here are some reasons why your organization—and your people—should embrace innovation. You can probably think of more!

1. Technology is constantly advancing, and our products need to keep pace.

2. Our customers have other choices from our competitors. We want to stay number one in the minds of our customers and keep them coming to us.

3. If we innovate, we can charge more for our products, and make more money.

4. We want to hire the best talent. Smart, aggressive people don't like to sit around and do the same things year after year. They want to be challenged.

5. We're human beings, and we like to explore. Exploration leads to innovation, which leads to economic growth.

How many more reasons can you think of?

2. The Vision

From your answers to the question of "Why innovate?" comes your vision for innovation. It should be written out, like an organizational mission or vision statement that focuses on innovation.

And to answer the question, "Why should we have a vision for innovation?" here are three benefits of having a vision that's clear and concise:

1. **Engagement.** With a clear innovation vision, stakeholders will share a common goal and have a sense of being on a journey together. They will be less likely to waste time on nonproductive activities. They'll be more willing to accept the difficulties, challenges, and changes that the innovation journey can entail.

2. **Responsibility.** The innovation vision guides the innovation systems, which in turn manage the innovative pipeline and its various initiatives. With a vision and systems in place, staff can be empowered and given more leeway in their work. Because they know the goals and direction toward which they are working, they can be trusted to steer their own ship and determine the best way of getting there.

3. **Creativity.** If people know there are unsolved challenges lying ahead, they'll be more creative and willing to contribute more ideas. Because they've bought into the journey, they'll be more motivated to find ways to go over and around the obstacles in their paths.

Here's what Satya Nadella wrote in 2014, a few months after he took over as CEO of Microsoft: "The day I took on my new role I said that our industry does not respect tradition—it only respects innovation. I also said that in order to accelerate our innovation, we must rediscover our soul—our unique core."[2]

But lest you think Nadella was concerned only with big-picture, philosophical matters, later in his memo he got very much down to earth: "We help people get stuff done. Stuff like term papers, recipes, and budgets. Stuff like chatting with friends and family across the world. Stuff like painting, writing poetry, and expressing ideas. Stuff like running a Formula 1 racing team or keeping an entire city running. Stuff like building a game with a spark of your imagination and remixing it with the world. And stuff like helping build a vaccine for HIV, and giving a voice to the voiceless."

As with a strategic plan, the best innovation operating systems have the vision of innovation at the very top. This is important because a vision, being both intellectual and emotional, should be easy to communicate. You should be thoughtful in the creation of your vision statement, as this is something you will use to communicate to both internal- and external-facing customers. Just as you did when you asked the question "why?" don't go it alone! Make the process of forming your innovation vision open and transparent. Solicit stakeholder input. Generate a series of drafts, tear them up, and write some more.

The innovation vision must be powerful and transformative, and deserve the full support of every stakeholder. It must be fully embraced and championed by leadership. As former General Electric CEO Jack Welch said, "Good business leaders create a vision, articulate the vision, passionately own the vision, and relentlessly drive it to completion."[3]

Remember that a vision statement isn't the same thing as a mission statement. While a mission statement describes what a company wants to do *now*, a vision statement outlines what a company wants to be *in the future*. It can also describe what kind of world it wants to help create for the future.

That being said, some companies blur the distinction. By whatever name you call it, the important thing is to *create it* and *communicate it*!

Here are a few examples. I've added the emphasis:

"Bring inspiration and **innovation** to every athlete* in the world. (*If you have a body, you are an athlete.)"—Nike

"To offer travelers a reliable, **innovative**, and fun airline to travel in Central America."—NatureAir

"Our mission is to make Target your preferred shopping destination in all channels by delivering outstanding value, continuous **innovation**, and exceptional guest experiences by consistently fulfilling our Expect More. Pay Less. Brand Promise."—Target

"We believe that we are on the face of the earth to make great products and that's not changing. We are constantly focusing on **innovating**. We believe in the simple not the complex. . . . We believe in deep collaboration and cross-pollination of our groups, which allow us to **innovate** in a way that others cannot."—Apple Computer

"Digital currency will bring about more **innovation**, efficiency, and equality of opportunity in the world by creating an open financial system."—Coinbase

"At Philips, we strive to make the world healthier and more sustainable through **innovation**. Our goal is to improve the lives of 3 billion people a year by 2025. We improve the quality of people's lives through technology-enabled meaningful **innovations**." – Philips Research

"Offering all women and men worldwide the best of cosmetics **innovation** in terms of quality, efficacy, and safety."—L'Oreal

"Using our portfolio of brands to differentiate our content, services, and consumer products, we seek to develop the most creative, **innovative**, and profitable entertainment experiences and related products in the world."—Disney Corporation

"To be the most **innovative** enterprise in the world."—3M[4]

Because innovation is unpredictable, don't box yourself out of opportunities by being too specific with your vision statement. Organizations should, however, be big, brave, and bold in their vision statement and their innovation initiative alike.

Also, please note that while you typically create your innovation vision early in the process, you can do it anytime. Formulating a vision often takes time, so you may start the process and then continue it while you work through the other steps. And, your organizational mission and vision statements should be reviewed once every few years to ensure they're still exactly what you want and are relevant. It's not uncommon for organizations to rewrite or revise their mission and vision statements as conditions change.

3. The Definition

Once you've determined why you're creating your Innovation Mandate and have a vision for your outcome or for the world as you hope to make it, you will then be well suited to begin the process of defining what it is and how it moves you toward your organizational goal. The definition should be understandable, relevant to your organization, and, most importantly, measurable and attainable.

Here's where a *gap analysis* is very useful.

A gap analysis involves the comparison of actual performance with potential or desired performance. It involves determining, documenting, and improving the difference between business requirements and current capabilities. It's a formal study of what a business is doing currently and where it wants to go in the future.

Please note that the capitalized "GAP analysis" has also been used as a means of classifying how well a product or solution meets a targeted need or set of requirements. In this case, the acronym GAP can be used as a ranking of "good," "average," or "poor."

In everyday business, a gap analysis can be used to define what it will take to meet a goal. Here's a simple example:

1. Identify the status quo: We're selling 5,000 units per month at a net profit of $1 million.

2. Identify the target: We want to net $1.5 million within two years.

3. How can we reach the target?
   A. Cut our expenses so we can sell 5,000 units but net $1.5 million.
   B. Sell 7,500 units of the same product at the same price.
   C. Raise the price per unit by selling an innovative model with more features.
   D. A combination of A, B, and C.

4. Challenges.
   A. We believe our existing geographical market is saturated, and we're not ready to expand into a new market.
   B. Our factory is at 100 percent capacity and we can't expand before two years.

5. Strategy: We will seek to bridge the gap by *innovating* and making our product a *better value* so that customers will pay more for it.

You can define what you want to get from innovation and set appropriate and attainable goals. Here are just a few examples:

- Mandate that a certain percentage of annual revenues must come from new products. This is often called the "innovation sales rate" (ISR).
- Track how many ideas per month you're getting from all of your employees.
- Measure the success of individual innovation projects (from concept to customer) and overall platform or new business development programs.
- Calculate the risk-adjusted net present value of the innovation pipeline and the return on investment in that pipeline. I'll talk about the innovation pipeline in the pages ahead.

Remember that inherent in innovation is exploring the unknown, and that brings with it an expected rate of failure. Accordingly, it's important to measure innovation holistically. Each individual effort cannot and should not be measured at the innovation state. Beware of measuring only what's *easy* to measure instead of what's *important*, and avoid measuring too many things.

4. The Readiness Assessment

Innovation is a people-powered process. Innovation is literally the process of gaining insights and ideas and putting them into action; and as of today, robots and computers aren't good at this. People must do it, and they need to be ready and willing.

Complete your assessment to determine how you will reach out to stakeholders, partners, vendors, customers, and in some cases even competitors, to get insights that you can transmute into organizational and customer value.

A gap analysis isn't just for the operational stuff. It can also be useful when looking at the readiness of your leaders and employees.

For example, in 2015, the Korn Ferry Institute conducted a side-by-side comparison of a group of logistics executives from average companies and those from *Forbes* magazine's "The World's 100 Most Innovative Companies." The study was based on the premise that if innovation were crucial to successful strategies across a company's supply chain, then logistics sector leaders needed to possess the personal qualities that would enable the spark of innovation to flourish.

The study found that when compared to their MIC peers, the group of average logistics executives "typically displayed lower levels of learning agility and cultural dexterity—two traits highly predictive of success and engagement, especially in senior leadership roles."

Learning agility is defined as the willingness and ability to learn from experience, and to then apply this knowledge to succeed under new or first-time conditions.

Cultural dexterity is defined as a professional's ability to work effectively with individuals from various cultural backgrounds.

Both are important for sustained innovation.

The Institute reported the average logistics leaders excelled in only one among eleven innovation indicators—independence. Meanwhile, executives in the *Forbes* MIC received top scores of ten in seven areas: cultural dexterity, learning agility, emotional intelligence, self, power, challenge, and independence, and scored nine in thought, which has a specific innovation component.

Overall, the *Forbes* MIC executives outperformed the average logistics leaders by nearly 50 percent.[5]

This is not surprising!

The embrace of innovation must be well thought out and sustained.

Here's some tough love: stocking your employee lounge with Ping-Pong tables, installing whiteboards, hosting quarterly hackathons, and proclaiming casual Fridays isn't the way to ensure innovation readiness! Leaders often seize upon these quick-fix tactics and convince themselves they are ready for innovation when, in fact, the critical ingredients of innovation are missing.

Instead, survey your managers and employees and ask them if they can define the *problem* they're solving for the customer. You don't want them to describe the current solution. You don't want them to say, "We make a great product." That means they're only thinking about today. If they're focused on the *problem*, they'll be thinking about how to create better solutions for the future.

When your people are ready for the spark of innovation, they'll capture it and harness its tremendous energy.

5. The Team Architecture

Your Innovation Mandate needs to be both well defined and flexible.

Strong but able to bend.

Identifiable but shape shifting.

And while it needs to be democratic and woven into the fabric of your organization at every level, like any other operational function it requires guidance and oversight.

While everyone in your organization should *participate* in innovation, you don't need an organization full of innovation directors. It's no different from, say, quality control. While everyone in an organization should support and pursue the highest standards of quality control, you don't want them all to be quality-control officers. You need people who can oversee and evaluate your innovation program, just like any other operational area of the organization.

If your organization is large, you may have multiple innovation teams. Most teams will appoint a team leader, who is responsible for establishing process, including how to communicate during brainstorms and meetings. That person can also help guide to the top of the organization the ideas and initiatives introduced in those meetings.

At the very least, you need an *innovation champion*. In a small company it could be the CEO, or in a larger organization there might be several. The innovation champion has the power to allocate resources within a set budget and ensure that the innovation pipeline is full.

CONTINUOUS IMPROVEMENT, BIG BREAKTHROUGHS . . . OR BOTH?

Innovation generally manifests itself in two ways:

1. **Continuous improvement.** This is the Japanese *kaizen*. Here, you're looking for a steady stream of small ideas from frontline workers in every department, which, when implemented, will deliver an incremental improvement to a process or product. To create and maintain this kind of approach, the only significant investment you need to make is in your *people*. They need to know they're *expected* to offer ideas, they need to know *how* to do it, and there needs to be a person or people who *receive* the ideas and process them.

   Hackathons are fine, but only as part of a long-term strategic embrace of innovation. If a hackathon is just a one-shot event, the end result will be worse than doing nothing because the employees will feel used.

2. **The big breakthrough**. This is what we see in structured innovation programs that have a specific project goal, such as to find a new drug to combat a particular disease. Big breakthroughs require line-item funding, staffing, and often a capital investment in space and equipment. The company looks for a return on investment, not necessarily from each specific project but from the innovation effort as a whole.

Many companies use a hybrid approach, and look for both continuous improvement as well as big breakthroughs.

YOUR PEOPLE ARE THE KEY

No matter how you organize your innovation effort, you must have people who are responsible for the entire innovation process.

Here are the key attributes of people you need on your innovation team:

- You need an innovation champion on the team who has access to the "go" button. This is absolutely key. If new ideas can't be propelled across the finish line, team members will quickly figure out they're nothing but empty window dressing.
- In architecting your innovation team, it's incredibly important that you leverage a thoughtful group of people who have the ability to provide real value in the assessment and development of innovations. You need subject experts in the relevant areas—marketing, design, production, human resources, finance.
- This is not about putting together a group of sycophants; in fact, you want a team that will likely get a bit scrappy given their wide range of views on all things innovation. Bring in a mix of veterans with deep experience of the core business but who may resist seeing new possibilities, along with younger "creatives" who are wired to generate crazy ideas that can't be implemented. Make them work together to recognize the spark and capture its full energy.
- The team members should be results-oriented, fast-moving, smart, and perhaps most importantly willing to take some big risks. You

don't want people who are comfortable simply punching the clock day after day.

- When working on a project basis, an effective group is comprised of individuals from different departments within the company. If the team's goal is to develop a new product, for example, there should be representatives from research and development, design, manufacturing, marketing, sales, and finance on board.

CODING YOUR INNOVATION OPERATING SYSTEM

Now that you have a reason *why* you need innovation, a *goal* that you want to achieve, and a *team* that will help you get there, it's time to build your plan—to write the operating code, so to speak.

Here's a winning structure you can use in the creation of your innovation operating system:

1. Establish a Clear Team and/or Organizational Process

Whether for a project team or the entire organization, a clear process ensures every employee can both participate in innovation and be held accountable to the same principles. Establish a leadership structure, define the roles of each team member, outline norms for how the team should collaborate, and set individual and group goals.

The more clarity and empowerment you can give the team and overall organization, the better.

2. Allocate Sufficient Resources

Like every functional area of your organization—human resources, operations, finance, compliance, logistics, marketing, or any other—innovation needs resources that will always include *time* and may also include *space*, *equipment*, and *information*.

Don't make innovation an also-ran. Because most team members aren't working solely on a single innovation project, employees are often pressured by other work demands. This is where the innovation champion is particularly useful—to give employees official permission to take chances or explore new ideas.

3. Encourage and Embrace Failure

Innovation and failure go hand in hand. That's to be expected.

Failure should mean that the team tried a new idea and learned an invaluable business lesson. For employees to believe that failure is okay, the organization needs to create a climate of "psychological safety"—a term coined by Harvard Business School professor Amy Edmondson. It's a work environment in which people feel comfortable admitting to well-intentioned mistakes without fear of being punished. What no one wants is a climate where mistakes are made and then covered up because team members don't want to be made to feel vulnerable.

Failure should be written into the budget. Unless a company is defined by its breakthrough products, the company's bottom line should never wholly depend upon the success of one risky project.

4. Ensure Employee Engagement

When innovation is a team or project effort, leaders need to ensure that everyone understands and supports the organization's commitment to innovation and that the team receives the cooperation it needs to succeed.

While in a large organization it's neither necessary nor desirable to plug every employee into the decision-making process, the more visibility innovators can bring to their work, the more willing other stakeholders will be to help and adopt new services, processes, or tools.

Making everyone comfortable with innovation is best done through personal conversation. Leaders need to lay out the vision, take questions, and get a sense of the organization's appetite for both incremental innovation and larger risks.

Before trying to make the big sell, innovation team members can gain a better understanding of the problems facing the organization and uncover any main points of objection they might face by meeting with other colleagues as well as the innovation champion.

Innovation is a series of concrete, definable actions. You don't have to be born with the ability to be innovative. Because it's a set of behaviors that can be learned, anyone is capable of doing it—that is, as long as the organization makes it a priority.

INNOVATION BY COLLABORATION:
THE LINUX OPERATING SYSTEM

Speaking of operating systems, one of the most innovative computer operating systems was the product of open collaboration. It all started in 1991 with the commencement of a personal project by Finnish student Linus Torvalds to create a new free operating system kernel. He initially called it "Freax," and he posted a public note that said, in part, "I'd like to know what features most people would want. Any suggestions are welcome, but I won't promise I'll implement them :-)."[6]

The initial governance structure of the Linux project required that all code be reviewed by Torvalds. This worked while the project was relatively small, but as the demand for Linux grew and the kernel became more and more complex, this structure simply wasn't sustainable.

The project quickly devolved into various subsystems, each with their own maintainer overseeing a specialized niche of the kernel, such as networking or file systems. Within each of these subsystems are additional submaintainers, who oversee even more specialized components. As a reflection of the logical scaling of the project, the decentralized approach works very well.[7]

The development of Linux is one of the most prominent examples of free and open-source software collaboration, in which underlying source code may be used, modified, and distributed—commercially or noncommercially—by anyone under the terms of its respective licenses, such as the GNU General Public License.

Today, the Linux Foundation pursues a mission of innovation, and says, "The Linux Foundation has taken its experience and expertise supporting the Linux community to help establish, build, and sustain some of the most critical open source technologies. Its work today extends far beyond Linux, fostering innovation in every layer of the software stack."[8]

To create your innovation operating system, follow the six steps:

1. **Why.**

    This is your compass that keeps you pointed toward your goal. Do not start until you know exactly why innovation will benefit your organization.

2. **Vision.**

    "See" the innovations you want to create. Not the innovations themselves, of course, but the problems you want to solve and how your organization could make a difference.

3. **Definition.**

    What kinds of innovation are you looking for? Incremental or breakthrough, or a combination? Process or product? Remember, innovations don't have to be directly experienced by the customer. For example, significant innovation is happening in logistics and human resources.

4. **Readiness.**

    Innovation is created and championed by people. Your leaders and your employees must be ready and willing to embrace innovation in all its forms.

5. **Architecture.**

Do you need defined teams to work on projects, or are you looking for every employee to offer ideas? Be sure to identify—and empower—as many innovation champions as you need.

6. **Coding.**

Establish the structure of your innovation program, with clear procedures and processes. These need to be both structured and flexible. Ensure buy-in from every relevant stakeholder.

9

THE INNOVATION PIPELINE

The first question leaders often ask is this: "Where does innovation spark?" And the second question is, "How do we manage it and make it profitable?" The answer to both questions is the innovation pipeline.

Pipelines in business are nothing new—here are three examples:

1. **A product pipeline** manages the development and marketing of new products. One of the clearest examples of product pipelines is in the pharmaceutical industry, where firms are constantly looking to develop new drugs for the market, and the process of development to sale goes through well-defined steps. You'll see robust product pipelines in consumer electronics, aerospace, the automotive industry, the entertainment industry—in fact, just about any industry where products have life cycles and new products must be developed to either replace the old ones or add to an existing product line.

2. **A leadership pipeline** is a standard feature in most large organizations. The recruiting, training, deploying, and reviewing of leaders is a necessary process for the long-term success of any company. A good leadership pipeline will manage every phase of leadership opportunities from new member to senior staff, and provide a detailed road map for each person interested in pursuing leadership within the organization.

3. **A sales pipeline** tracks and manages the life cycle of the customer experience, from initial interaction to closing the deal. These steps

include gathering incoming sales leads, qualifying prospects into sales-qualified leads, validating a qualified lead into a sales opportunity, and then registering the deal as closed, on hold, or lost. It also manages repeat customers and identifies opportunities to upsell them.

The expected outcomes of a sales pipeline are typically measured by four metrics:

1. The number of prospects or possible sales in the pipeline

2. The average size of a sale in the pipeline

3. The average close ratio, or the average percentage of sales that are made

4. Sales velocity, meaning the average amount of time it takes to make a sale. This is important, because, all other factors being equal, making ten sales per day is obviously better than making one sale per day.

It's easy to see that if you're in business, you already know the importance of pipelines! An innovation pipeline is no different. It has a purpose and a structure, and there are ways to measure its effectiveness. All you need to do is transfer what you already know about business pipelines to the realm of innovation.

WHERE INNOVATION SPARKS

But let's go back to the first question: "Where does innovation spark?"

In the first chapter of this book, we discussed this important topic. Innovation can spark in many places and under a wide variety of conditions. They include:

1. **From the lab.** In many companies, innovation is meticulously planned, and typically takes the form of an effort to find a solution for a specific, known problem. This is particularly true in pharmaceutical companies, where bringing a new drug to market takes a huge investment in time and money.

But planned innovations aren't just expensive R&D programs. Toyota's Creative Idea and Suggestion System is a form of planned innovation in which the rate of spontaneous new ideas has become predictable, and while the exact ideas are not known until they're submitted, the overall idea flow is entirely planned and has been formalized into the company's operations.[1]

2. **Out of the blue**. These are unplanned breakthroughs or new ideas that defy prediction. In familiar industries, many examples have become legendary. But unexpected innovation can happen anywhere. Take musical theater—not always innovative, and always risky. By bringing the rhythms and attitude of hip-hop to the otherwise stodgy historical biography of Alexander Hamilton, composer, lyricist, and actor Lin-Manuel Miranda created an electrifying crossover product in the form of *Hamilton*, the hit musical that is consistently selling out and bringing in nearly $100 million a year in gross revenues. To date, on an initial investment of about $12.5 million, the show's investors have made unprecedented returns of roughly 600 percent![2]

Hip-hop music and the Founding Fathers—who would have guessed?

3. **Collaboration with partners.** Companies are increasingly regarding stakeholders as partners in new product or service development. Customers, suppliers, and end-users often have significant skills and knowledge that can be leveraged for innovation development.

Organizations are beginning to cocreate with brands from other markets to create an opportunity for the respective businesses and the customers they serve. Successful brand collaboration depends on both brands benefitting from the existing market of the other, or by filling an opening in the market through a collaborative relationship.

Many organizations are building innovation spaces where they actually spend a great deal of time with their customers and users to significantly improve their product offering and create new and exciting customer-centric innovations.

4. **Crowdsourcing.** With the rise of the internet as a reliable global platform, we've seen the emergence of company interactions with external crowds on innovation projects in diverse business areas. Crowdsourcing can take the form of contests, collaborative communities, complementors, or freelance labor markets. Each one has its own characteristics and strong points.

5. **Open innovation.** Promoted by Henry Chesbrough in his book *Open Innovation: The New Imperative for Creating and Profiting from Technology*, open innovation requires that innovators integrate their ideas, expertise, and skills with those of others outside the organization to deliver the result to the marketplace, using the most effective means possible.[3]

Does managing innovation seem like herding cats?

Perhaps. But it doesn't have to!

You just need to be organized and have a robust innovation pipeline.

THE STRATEGIC CASE

In building an innovation pipeline, the first step is to know two things:

1. Why you're doing it
2. What you hope to get out of it

The strategic case is at the very core of the innovation process. It provides guidance on what an organization wants to achieve with innovation. It includes high-level technology, market, and industry assessments. Strategic analysis is not to be confused with market research, as the latter includes more focused investigation of market size and market segments.

An innovation effort may be carefully planned to find a solution for a known problem, such as developing a drug to fight a certain disease.

It may have the goal of finding unexpected and unforeseen innovations, either as products or as process innovations that either save the company money or add value for the customer.

Whatever it is, at the end of the day any innovation must satisfy our ironclad definition:

**Innovation is the creation of new value that serves
your organization's mission and customer.**

Your innovation pipeline will consist of five phases that enable your organization to identify, capture, validate, develop, and deploy the new ideas that will keep you highly relevant to your market and ahead of the competition.

The five phases are:

1. The Spark Generator
2. Fast Filter
3. The Messy Middle
4. Octagon Optimization
5. The Perfect Plan

Let's explore them!

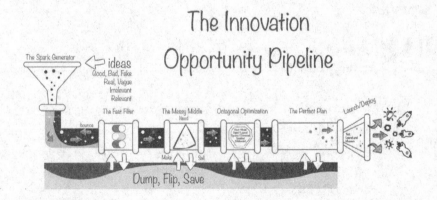

1. The Spark Generator

Have you ever seen someone welding or fabricating steel, and the sparks are flying in every direction?

That's what you want. At the entrance to your innovation pipeline, you want to see a cloud of dancing, brilliant sparks, coming from all directions and bouncing off each other. Some fly off into space, but many of them enter the pipeline.

Here at the entrance, all sparks are created equal. They come from the employee suggestion box, from customer comments on social media, from vendors, from competitors (the ideas you steal!), from the R&D people in the lab. No idea has any more validity than another.

In the world of project management, this is the "brainstorming" level. It's where the team leader calls for ideas from everyone, and in a mad rush writes them all down on the whiteboard without thinking about them.

In the spark generator, quantity equals quality. The more the merrier! You want sparks flying like embers from a roaring bonfire, lighting up the night.

MEASURING THE INPUT

While the spark generator is a wild and untamed frontier, like everything else in business its performance needs to be measured. You need to know how many possible sparks can be collected during a given period of time, and how efficiently your pipeline is collecting sparks for processing.

In any business measurement, of course, three metrics are the most important:

1. Over time, are your results trending up (good!), staying flat (okay), or trending down (bad)?

2. Do your results meet your goal? If not, is your goal too high, or is performance too low?

3. How do you measure up against the marketplace and the competition? Are you a leader or a follower?

As you will see when you switch on your innovation pipeline and set innovation goals, you'll need time for your results to "normalize." As time passes, you may need to adjust your pipeline to meet the reality of what your organization can achieve. That's perfectly okay!

There are many ways to measure the input into your innovation pipeline. Here are just a few:

1. **Number of employee suggestions per week or month.** This is perhaps the simplest metric, in which you solicit and then count the number of suggestions from employees. The ubiquitous employee suggestion box is a good example. There is virtually no upfront capital investment required other than the time the innovation champion or team spends collecting and reviewing the suggestions.

2. **Number of customer comments and suggestions.** Listen to your customers, *especially* the unhappy ones who complain on social media or review sites. Make sure your social media people reply to or acknowledge every comment or question. Your customers are giving you free insights and advice, which is cheaper than paying a consultant and probably more useful!

   As Molly St. Louis wrote for *Inc.* magazine, Citibank aggressively courts its customers, and the feedback pays off. For example, from its customers the bank realized that mobile banking was spreading and becoming increasingly important to their customers. In response, the bank honed its user-friendly app, and in 2016 saw mobile banking increase by 50 percent and the number of downloaded apps double.[4]

3. **Number of new inventions or products coming from your R&D labs.** This is a straight ROI situation, and can be managed like any other functional area. The key is to properly recognize an innovation that can make a difference in the future, not just right now.

   For example, in 1975, Steven Sasson, a young engineer at Eastman Kodak, invented the first working digital camera. It was an ungainly device, but it worked.

   Kodak executives were not interested.

   Then in 1989, Sasson and a colleague, Robert Hills, created the first modern digital single-lens reflex (SLR) camera that looked and functioned like a normal camera. It had a 1.2 megapixel sensor, and used image compression and memory cards.

   The Kodak brass were still unconvinced. They didn't want to undercut their sales of old-fashioned film. As Sasson told the *New York Times*, "Of course, the problem is pretty soon you won't be able to sell film—and that was my position."

While Kodak licensed its digital technology to other companies, for its own products it clung to its outdated business model and failed to ride the massive market disruption of digital cameras.

In January 2012, the company filed for Chapter 11 bankruptcy.[5]

Don't let this happen to you!

4. **Number of innovations licensed from other companies**. See #3, above. Apple's pioneering QuickTake consumer digital camera, introduced in 1994, had the Apple label but was produced by Kodak. *Time* magazine called QuickTake "the first consumer digital camera." When Apple couldn't do something in-house, the company acquired innovation from third parties.[6]

5. **Number of ideas from other sources including contests**. Google "innovation contest winner" and you'll get thirty million results! The idea is nothing new. One of the most historically significant crowdsourcing innovation contests was announced in London in 1714. The Longitude Act, administered by the Board of Longitude, sought solutions to the problem of determining a ship's location on the open sea, out of sight of land. The contest ran for 114 years, and many rewards were paid out to individuals who offered verifiable improvements over existing methods.

Today, contests and other crowdsourcing methods are a significant source of new ideas for organizations of all types and sizes. They can be internal or open. In 2015, drug maker Pfizer used an internal innovation challenge to help create a new mobile tool for patients seeking to stop smoking. The company created a *Shark Tank*–style competition for its brand teams, which generated roughly one hundred ideas. The winning idea was an unbranded mobile smoking-cessation app developed with the American Lung Association.[7]

2. The Fast Filter

Now that you've got a shower of bright sparks flying around the spark generator of your innovation pipeline, what's next?

How do you begin to evaluate and sort them, separating the ones that have potential from the ones that are obviously worthless?

This is a critically important phase. Why? Because it's easy to either throw out ideas that are good or waste time on ideas that are bad. No one wants to do that!

Some organizations receive thousands of innovation submissions each year, and they are so backlogged that there is literally no way they will ever catch up. Sadly, in those piles of unexamined innovations, market-leading and enterprise-beneficial ideas are hiding. It's like leaving money on the table.

As the name suggests, the fast filter must have two key attributes:

1. Speed. You need a system for quickly evaluating each idea, rendering a decision, and either discarding it or letting it pass through.

2. Accuracy. You need a system that will retain good ideas and reject bad ideas.

FLOW MANAGEMENT: THE TOGGLE SYSTEM

If you've ever seen a dam on a river, you know that a dam serves two functions: it holds back the great mass of water while letting a controlled amount of water get through. The water that is allowed to get through provides value, often in the form of hydroelectric power or irrigating farms downstream.

Your innovation pipeline is no different. You set up a series of controls to both manage the flow and develop the value of the ideas that you allow to proceed downstream.

Instead of dams, you could think in terms of toggle switches. Once you've done the heavy lifting of determining what you want, you can then easily set up binary "yes/no" toggles to determine if an innovation makes sense for you to even look at. This automates the most painful parts of innovation, which are sifting through the sand to find that one nugget of gold and then dealing with disappointed innovators.

Each toggle has two positions:

1. Discard the idea. In all probability, 80 percent of all ideas entering the fast filter will be rejected instantly. This is because either they don't fit the established guidelines for acceptance (such as criteria for new inventions), or the innovation champion has reviewed them and found them obviously unsuitable or irrelevant.

2. Let the idea pass through because you accept it, or it needs more study, or it's temporarily archived for later use. These will comprise about 20 percent of the ideas entering the fast filter.

As you can see, toggle position number two is nuanced.

Of all the ideas allowed to pass through, perhaps just one in ten will be immediately accepted. These will be ideas that:

- *Are super-simple, inexpensive, and obviously good.* Take, for example, the idea cited earlier in this book about British Airways descaling the toilet pipes on its planes, thus making them lighter. This is the type of idea where you smack yourself on the forehead and say, "Why didn't we think of that before now?"
- *Totally fit an agreed-upon set of criteria.* Let's say you're looking for a new device to solve a problem on your production line, and a supplier responds with exactly what you need. Case closed.

The remaining 90 percent of ideas allowed to pass through the filter will need more study. Most ideas that you get will be incomplete, simply because they're narrow solutions to a problem and the organizational ramifications haven't been researched. For example, if someone suggests that you adopt a policy of flexible hours for your employees, if the idea seems appealing you're going to want to study it carefully before making a decision.

TOGGLES: MANUAL OR AUTOMATED

The toggles are placed at every phase of the pipeline, from the spark generator all the way to the back end where the final decisions are made to keep or shelve an idea, product, or process. As we've seen in case studies such as the General Motors EV1 electric car, which was scrapped after 1,117 cars were built and leased to customers, the "kill" toggle can be located at the very end of the innovation pipeline, after significant investment has been made.[8]

However, the highest concentration of toggles will be found in the fast filter. This is simply because here the volume of ideas is the greatest and their variety the most extreme, and there's the most urgency to separate the wheat from the chaff. In fact, the fast filter is nothing but a collection of toggles. That's its only function.

Toggles can be either thrown manually or automated. Either way, the decision must be made based upon a set of predetermined rules followed either by a human being (innovation champion or committee) or a software program.

The idea of an automated toggle system should be familiar to anyone who has either worked in human resources in a big company or applied for a job at a big company. When advertising open positions, such organizations can receive thousands of résumés, and many employ digital applicant tracking systems as the first set of toggles. The scanning software looks for keywords in a résumé that match keywords used in the job description. So if you apply for a job as a software engineer and the job posting says they want experience with "middleware Java stack," if your résumé doesn't include the words "middleware Java stack," it will be rejected.

Your innovation pipeline toggles can perform the same function. They can be completely customized to connect to a screening process, thereby allowing an organization to screen thousands of submissions without ever actually looking at the submissions.

3. The Messy Middle

Entering the messy middle are the sparks that have blazed their way through the spark generator and survived the fast filter. These are the ideas that are worth a small investment in time or resources to determine their value.

The messy middle is the complex and amorphous process of closely examining an innovation to determine if it has a chance of delivering value to your organization, your mission, and ultimately your customer.

I've developed an exclusive program I humbly call WebbLogic that takes a three-dimensional approach toward evaluating the three most important aspects of innovation.

THE WEBBLOGIC MODEL

The biggest problem of most innovation evaluation tools is that they are 100 percent *risk centric*. They are more correctly seen as *innovation prevention* approaches. New ideas are judged solely on the basis of risk, and the higher the perceived risk—regardless of the possible benefit—the greater pressure there is to reject the idea and stick with the status quo.

There's a better way to evaluate innovations.

Before you evaluate the suitability of an innovation for your organization, market, and customer, you must begin with your strategic case, which consists of the answers to as many of these key questions as apply to your organization:

- What does our customer want?
- What are the key competitive trends?
- What are the new enabling technologies that we can leverage?
- How much money do we have to develop and commercialize an idea?
- Does the new innovation square up with our organizational mission and strategies?
- Can we really deliver an innovation that provides exceptional market and customer value?
- Do we have the internal skill sets to evaluate the idea?
- Do we have all the information we need to determine if an idea is good?
- Do we have the team architecture to make the right choice on moving ideas forward?

This is just a small sampling of the possible questions that need to be answered as part of your overarching strategic case. Because your organization is unique, your strategic case will be tailored to your needs.

The WebbLogic model is a triangle consisting of a center plus three key areas of assessment.

The WebbLogic Triangle

Opportunity

At the top point of the triangle is **Opportunity**.

The best innovations meet a specific need or solve a problem. This creates an opportunity. Need or problem = opportunity. Without this you don't have an idea.

One of the most common mistakes is making assumptions about an opportunity. Often organizations don't gather sufficient information to determine whether a perceived need is widely recognized or even big enough to constitute a viable marketplace. In the old days we used to use a system called voice of the customer (VOC) to get information from potential customers as to whether they'd be interested in buying a product if the company actually made it. The problem is that it's easy for a person being polled to say yes when they're not being asked to actually spend money, so oftentimes organizations would get erroneous feedback about the potential marketability of a product or service. We need to go far beyond these old-fashioned risk-centric methods to really drill down to understand not the voice of the customer but rather *the soul of the customer* (SOC). We don't care what they say or even what they think—what we really care about is what they *believe* and ultimately what they will *do*.

Sell

In the lower left-hand corner of the triangle is **Sell**.

Surprisingly, many innovators make broad and baseless assumptions about the marketability of an idea. The hysteria around an organization's or inventor's belief in the marketability of their idea can be astonishing. You need to be coldly objective about any idea that comes along, including your own.

I must confess I'm guilty of doing exactly what I'm asking you to avoid! A few years back I had the brilliant idea to take half a million dollars from my children's college fund and invest it into an inflatable abdominal exercise device. I believed the risk was low, so I decided to do it. The product, Astro Abs, was to be sold on a single, one-time-only TV infomercial scheduled to air on a Saturday night. The commercial was expensive and beautifully filmed. I thought it was practically a work of art.

I'll never forget that Sunday morning when the producer of the infomercial called me. I was standing in my backyard watching my five-year-old daughter,

Taylor, swimming in the pool and having the time of her life. I heard the phone ring in the house. This was it—the call that would confirm my tremendous success! My wife, who was in the house, answered the phone. Then she came outside, phone in hand. On her face was a strange, stricken expression. Still expecting positive news, I took the phone from her.

In a somber voice, the producer said, "Sorry, Nick—it's done."

"What do you mean, 'It's done'?"

"The infomercial was a total flop. No one wanted the product. We sold nothing."

Stunned, I thanked him and clicked off the phone. I had lost my entire investment. He did not see a way to resurrect the commercial messaging or the product. There would be no retest, no second opportunity.

I looked at my daughter and thought to myself, *Oh my God, I just threw away your college fund!*

Eventually I was able to replace her college fund, and in many ways this was possible because of the very lessons I had learned from that mistake.

The takeaway here is pretty simple: *Fall out of love with your brilliant idea.*

Love is an irrational emotion that will prevent you from honestly evaluating the marketability of your idea. Had I completed my due diligence on the inflatable abdominal exercise device, I would have been able to identify the problems and circumvent a major financial hit. You need to know if an idea will sell!

Many organizations conduct sterile research to draw conclusions about the marketability of a technology or service. A far better way is to actually ask someone to buy it *now*. Asking someone if they're interested in the technology or service versus having them sign on the dotted line is quite a different thing. Take, for example, the crowdfunding site Kickstarter, which sells ideas to early adopters before entering production or even finishing the prototype. The old-fashioned way that we used to determine the market viability of a product is simply deficient, especially given the access to far better and more accurate information sources. Today we can instantly find out vital information, such as:

- The size of the market
- Online success and failure stories about similar products
- Industry trends that impact the marketability of a product

- Deep insights through online social networks
- Insights from social ratings and other empirical customer communities

Build

In the lower right-hand corner of the triangle is **Build**.

It's safe to say that if you could build a perpetual motion machine, you'd be very successful in selling it. The problem is pesky old physics: a perpetual motion machine is a unicorn and will never be invented. It's just against the laws of nature.

There are two questions you need to ask for every innovative product:

1. **"Can we build it?"** This question can be significant—just ask Elon Musk, who with his company SpaceX is endeavoring to build reusable rockets that will land safely on Earth after boosting their payload into space. But other innovations may face a variety of obstacles, including, "Is it legal for us to build it?" and "Is it dangerous to build it?"

   Consider ABC Medical Device Company, which fabricates tools out of stainless steel. Someone at the company comes up with an amazing innovative device that's made out of plastic. The question of "Can we build it?" may then be a matter of current operational capability. ABC Medical Device doesn't fabricate tools out of plastic, only stainless steel; so no matter how awesome a suggestion may be for an innovative plastic instrument, it's not getting built by ABC Medical Device.

   But then again . . . Perhaps *because* of this suggested innovation, the leaders of ABC Medical Device should look at their business plan and consider whether expanding the business to include plastic fabrication would be a smart move. Is the market for plastic tools growing? What would it cost to enter it? Are the customers the same for stainless steel as they are for plastic? Should ABC enter into an agreement with an external plastic fabricator and sell the products under the ABC brand? These are all very good questions.

2. **"Can we *afford* to build it?"** The WebbLogic model forces you to evaluate whether your new service idea, enterprise innovation idea, or product can be built in a way that can successfully launch to a marketplace. When we think about the build corner of the model, we have to remember that there is always a need to look at *price sensitivity*. In other words, what the customer is willing to pay. You can build just about anything, but if the customer doesn't value it at the price you can afford to sell it, it will fail miserably. You need to ask yourself, "Can we effectively build this innovation in a way that provides differentiated value when compared to competitive options?" Don't just speculate about this. Verify it with experts. Get real quotes and work with real numbers. If you can't build it in a way that exceeds customer expectations and addresses price sensitivity, you don't have an idea.

The WebbLogic model can be adapted for use with innovations that impact processes rather than products—processes that are designed to cut costs or improve the quality of existing products and how they're produced.

Potential

In the center, or at the very heart, of the WebbLogic triangle is **Potential**.

The idea may look promising now, or it may look insignificant. The real question is, "What's its potential for growth and added value?"

Potential is the combination of the three points of the triangle: opportunity, build, and sell. Together they create potential, or lack thereof. An idea that lacks the potential to add value at a cost that will raise profits needs to be discarded. An idea that can add both value and profits deserves to be toggled through to the next section of the innovation pipeline.

The WebbLogic model can help you evaluate an innovation as well as guide you as you develop your criteria for your messy middle, where you take a closer look at eligible innovations to determine their financial and operational feasibility.

The ideas that fail the WebbLogic model get toggled out.

The ideas that show promise get toggled through.

4. Octagonal Optimization

Octagonal Optimization

Here we advance from the general to the particular.

We take a possible innovation and put it into our *business context*.

We know that innovation is a numbers game: the more sparks you have, the greater chance there is that one of them will blaze brightly into a brilliant star. Most sparks will fizzle out and disappear, but that's all right. It's just like hiring someone to fill a key role in your company: you may receive a hundred résumés, out of which you'll interview five candidates and ultimately hire just one. That's one in one hundred—which is fine, and what everyone expects. It's the way you find the best people!

Here in octagonal optimization, we strive to further clarify, identify, and strengthen those innovations that have entered the spark generator and passed through both the fast filter and the messy middle. Now we're getting to the best of the best! But the failure rate is still very high, just like when you're hiring for a key position. You know the old saying, "Hire slow, fire fast." The same applies to your innovation pipeline. Slowly nurture the sparks that may burn bright. The duds? Get rid of them quickly!

Now is the time to put the new ideas to the test and see where they fit into your business and its mission. Here are the eight areas where you can significantly improve your innovations and their odds of surviving:

1. **Plus it.** This is a phrase made famous by Walt Disney. When one of his Imagineers came up with an idea, Disney would say, "Interesting. Now plus it!" It was his way of asking them to take an idea and see how it

could be taken to the next level. Could it provide even more value? Be used in some other context? Create synergy with some other idea?

When talking about Disneyland, Disney said, "The park means a lot to me in that it's something that will never be finished. Something that I can keep developing, keep plussing and adding to—it's alive. It will be a live, breathing thing that will need changes. . . . I wanted something live, something that could grow, something I could keep plussing with ideas, you see?"[9]

2. **Model it.** Some of the best innovations today are not so much bright shiny objects but rather integrated business models. Can you optimize the idea by looking at the way in which you build out the commercial model? In other words, is the innovation utterly unique to your organization or even to one application, or can it be used to create value elsewhere?

It can be useful to create a minimally viable product (MVP), an early version of the product or service that envisages an interaction with a customer, stakeholder, or business process. Not only might this validate the idea, but by performing a quick initial and low-cost test you can assess what you're doing and decide whether to toggle the idea forward or jettison it.

3. **Digitize it.** It seems like everything today is either digital or digitally connected. Can your innovation become part of the digital universe to improve the way in which you can deliver value to your enterprise and customer? For example, in the innovation pipeline at ABC Medical Device is a new design for a stainless-steel refrigerator for storing vaccines. What will get the idea toggled through to the next phase is the fact that it can be digitally connected to the hospital's computer network and its inventory constantly monitored. Its compatibility with the Internet of Things (IoT) gives the design much greater value than simply being a good refrigerator.

4. **Layer it.** For a new product, layering value suggests that you add multiple layers of value in the way you design the packaging, warranties, and instructions. Every aspect of the innovation should have multiple

layers of value; often this involves little or no cost but makes a tremendous customer impact.

Layering has become ubiquitous in the automobile industry. In the past decade, much of the innovation in auto design has been in the realm of digital services for the driver and passengers: features including mobile communications, autonomous driving, remote self-starting, and vehicle systems monitoring have turned even low-priced automobiles into enormously complex digital machines.

For an organization that provides services, layering gives a critical competitive edge. If you're a marketing company, you may specialize in one core area, such as email marketing, but also have expertise in other areas such as SEO, website design, content marketing, or social media marketing. If a potential innovation can work across several layers, that's a strong asset. An innovation may also involve partnering with outside consultants who possess skills complementary to what you're offering; they can help you expand your market reach while taking some of the work off your hands.

5. **Make it dynamic.** If you have an Apple iPhone, then every once in a while you'll suddenly discover that your phone has magically gotten better. The iPhone is part of an open community of iPhone app developers that are constantly creating solutions that make the user's life easier and just plain better.

    Give your technology a way to continually evolve.

    But this doesn't just refer to the product itself. Sometimes the product "is what it is," and the dynamism comes in how you manufacture it or sell it. Earlier in the book we told the story of Febreze, the air freshener created by Proctor & Gamble. The product itself was innovative, which they thought was enough, and the company tried to sell it like any other air freshener. But consumers didn't respond. Eventually the *marketing campaign* became innovative and dynamic. By taking a new approach to selling the product, sales skyrocketed.

    Likewise, the Coca-Cola soft drink is the same product the company has been selling since 1886—and, in fact, consumers resist *any* change to the drink's formula! To keep pace with a rapidly evolving market, the company changes how they package and sell the product.

They also model it by manufacturing endless variations of the core product, including plain water, which is sold under the seemingly exotic name Dasani. In fact, Coca-Cola uses tap water from local municipal water supplies, which it then makes more palatable by filtering and adding trace minerals.[10]

6. **Connect it.** We are in a time of massive hyper-connectivity, and when anything can be connected, it will be connected; and when it's connected it will deliver more value. How can you build out connection architecture in your design?

   Nowhere is this seen better than in the way films and their interactive counterparts, video games, are marketed. The history of film and merchandising tie-ins dates back to 1925, with *The Lost World*. This American silent monster adventure film was released at the height of a "puzzle craze" in the United States, and plans were quickly drawn up to create marketing synergy. An innovative trailer was filmed showing cast members and the director poring over "The Lost World Puzzle," a simple set of twelve images that you needed to fit together.[11]

   The modern mega-tie-in template was forged in the 1990s, when director Steven Spielberg and Universal Pictures created enormous advertising and merchandising connections for his 1993 blockbuster *Jurassic Park*. During the pre-production phase that lasted over two years, Universal Studios inked over one hundred licensees to market over one thousand dinosaur products for the film. The big players were McDonald's, which invested $12 million; toymaker Kenner, which paid $8 million; and video-game company Sega, which contributed $7 million. It was the grand slam home run of film merchandising, with toys, video games, and cross-promotional tie-ins with big global brands.[12]

   Spawning four sequels in 1997, 2001, 2015, and 2018, *Jurassic Park* would reign atop the all-time worldwide box office for several years, earning over $900 million.

   The king of movie cross-marketing? As of the time of this writing, the Marvel Cinematic Universe, with its string of action-hero films, has posted worldwide gross receipts in excess of $14 billion.[13] Remember, the Marvel Cinematic Universe began in 1996 with a bankrupt comic book publishing company that made huge gambles—and won them all.[14]

Can an innovation in your pipeline be leveraged to create value in an unexpected way with a new connection?

7. **Socialize it.** Snapchat, Facebook, and Instagram have become ubiquitous. We are expected to be able to engage others with our connected devices, and we like to play social games and collaborate with others. Can your innovation be socialized so as to build a community of super-happy users?

For example, sportswear giant Nike has dialed back its television commercials, and instead pours its marketing resources into the digital space. The company uses social media to create a lifestyle and sense of community among consumers. Its tweets are concise and compelling, and nearly always include the hashtag #justdoit, as well as other community-building hashtags like #nikewomen. Nike has separate Facebook and Twitter accounts for each of its product categories, including golf, snowboarding, and FuelBand, as well as two football pages—one for the American variety and one for the variety played by everyone else in the world. And they're not just pushing product; the Nike Support feed resolves product questions and technical needs, and answers hundreds of questions per day.[15]

8. **Make it collaborative.** Never innovate in a vacuum! Find really smart people and even a few really crazy people to collaborate with you to look at an idea from many different vantage points. For example, if your innovation champion or committee is made up of people from logistics and production, they're going to look at every idea from their perspective. There's nothing wrong with this; it's just human nature. They will ask themselves, "How can we make this thing?" or "Will this idea cut costs?" They may miss how an innovation could make a big difference outside their area of responsibility.

A common obstacle to unexpected innovation is a cognitive bias that psychologists call "functional fixedness," which pioneering psychologist Karl Duncker defined as being a "mental block against using an object in a new way that is required to solve a problem." A company's leaders—and even its own innovation team—can't look beyond the way they have always looked for solutions. Ironically, success makes functional fixedness more ingrained; the more success a team has had with their standard approach to a problem, the more difficult it is to embrace one that is totally new and therefore perceived to be risky.

The most well-known example of functional fixedness is Duncker's story of the candle—which you can try yourself as a brain teaser. Participants were given a candle, a book of matches, and a small cardboard box containing a few thumbtacks. The challenge was to attach the candle to the wall and light it so the wax wouldn't drip on the table below.

Think about it for a moment. What's the solution?

Use the box as a candleholder by tacking it to the wall and setting the candle upright in the box.

Duncker theorized that participants who didn't figure it out were fixated on the box's normal function as a container for the thumbtacks and could not re-conceptualize it in a manner that allowed them to solve the problem.[16]

When an innovation arrives at the octagonal optimization phase, be sure to look at it with an open mind: it may have a function or value that you don't see right away!

5. The Perfect Plan

When an idea gets toggled through to this final phase, it's ready to be operationalized.

If it's a product, it needs to be manufactured and marketed.

If it's a process, it needs to be put into action.

To do this correctly requires a plan. Elements to be considered include:

- **Customer engagement.** If customers are directly involved, as with a product or a customer-facing process, then you need to identify them, reach them, get them excited, and get their feedback. With internal process innovations, such as an improvement to an assembly line, the "customers" are the employees impacted by the new process.
- **Channel plan.** You reach your customers through the paths or pipelines through which goods and services flow in one direction (from vendor to

the consumer), and the payments generated by them flow in the opposite direction (from consumer to the vendor).

- **Revenue and expense.** You want a return on the investment you're making in this new product or process. This applies to both selling a product and making an internal process innovation.
- **Marketing and communications.** You need to determine how you spend your marketing dollars and resources. Who will be responsible for the social media component?
- **Digital, social, and thought leadership.** Customers have opinions, as do reviewers and media partners. Increasingly, these opinions matter because anyone's viewpoint can be posted publicly in the digital town square.
- **Contingency plan.** If Plan A doesn't work the way you expected, you should have a Plan B in place that is something other than just killing the idea. This includes identifying alternative sources of funding, sourcing of raw materials, manufacturing, distribution, and marketing if the reality of the marketplace doesn't match your projections.
- **Integrated commercialization strategy.** This refers to the series of financing options that you consider as you move your technology or product from concept to the marketplace. You must estimate when your product will be commercially available, when your principal competitors are likely to enter the market (if they aren't already there), and when your target customers will become responsive to your technology or product.

THE INNOVATION PIPELINE OF XYZ CONTROLS COMPANY

Here's a super-simplified example of how an innovation pipeline can work.

The XYZ Controls Company makes and sells digital and mechanical control systems for big office buildings—equipment like HVAC systems, fire alarms, and security systems. It's a competitive market and the XYZ innovation pipeline is well established and productive.

Here's a table showing the fates of eight ideas that were vacuumed up into the pipeline.

Our table will begin with phase two—the fast filter. This is because the spark generator is nonjudgmental, and all ideas are accepted.

Phase 2	IDEA	EVALUATION	TOGGLE
1	Serve free lunch to employees	We're not Google	No
2	Sensor for room occupancy	Possible product innovation	Yes
3	Live chat website feature	Possible marketing innovation	Yes
4	Build another factory in Mexico	A very big question, but worth exploring	Yes
5	Give executives stock options	Looks too greedy	No
6	Install locks on office washrooms	Is this really a problem? Further study is requested.	Yes
7	New material for pipes	Possible product innovation	Yes
8	Explore nuclear fuel option	Crazy, but worth considering	Yes

As you can see, eight ideas have been collected by the spark generator, and they range from the obviously interesting to ideas that are more dubious. That's okay! This is the spark generator, and no idea is turned away. All are fed into the greedy mouth of the innovation pipeline. All are given a quick but fair evaluation.

In the fast filter, the organization's strategic case is applied—either manually or with software; it doesn't matter. Two ideas are rejected: free lunches and executive stock options.

Six ideas get a yes, meaning they go on to the next phase.

One idea—build another factory in Mexico—gets a "pass" because it's not a crazy idea but it requires a long-term analysis.

Two ideas get a flat no.

On to the next phase—the messy middle. This is where the WebbLogic model is applied. To make it simple, the bottom-line question is, "Does it pass the four criteria: potential, opportunity, sell, and build?" We'll call it POSB—yes or no.

Phase 3	IDEA	EVALUATION	TOGGLE
2	Sensor for room occupancy	POSB yes	Yes
3	Live chat website feature	POSB yes	Yes
4	Build another factory in Mexico	Needs further study by C-suite.	Yes
6	Install locks on washrooms	POSB no—HR reports there is no need for it.	No
7	New material for pipes	POSB yes	Yes
8	Explore nuclear fuel option	We cannot build this; there's no business case for acquiring the technology from a partner.	No

Here, two ideas get rejected because the innovation champion and other evaluators saw no POSB business case for toggling yes. As before, the idea of building another factory in Mexico has been toggled yes, not because it's accepted but because it requires significant study by top leaders. There are many innovations that the innovation champion and the relevant department heads can approve unilaterally; building a new factory is not one of them!

On to Phase 4—octagonal optimization. We have four ideas left.

Phase 4	IDEA	EVALUATION	TOGGLE
2	Sensor for room occupancy	Yes, commit funds	Yes
3	Live chat website feature	Yes, commit funds	Yes
4	Build another factory in Mexico	Yes, fund a study	Yes
7	New material for pipes	Modeling done—too expensive, not profitable, no business case.	No

Here we see that one idea—new material for pipes—has been judged not worth investing in. It's toggled no. But the committee decides to fund a study for building another factory in Mexico, so it's toggled yes. This does *not* mean it's going to happen, only that XYZ Controls Company has decided that the idea is worth exploring.

Next comes Phase 5—the perfect plan.

Phase 5	IDEA	EVALUATION	TOGGLE
2	Sensor for room occupancy	In development	Yes
3	Live chat website feature	In development	Yes
4	Build another factory in Mexico	Study ongoing	Pending

Out of the original batch of eight ideas, two are chosen to be put into service: the new sensor that detects how many people are in a room, and the website now has a live chat feature. The study of the factory in Mexico is ongoing.

Six months later, while the innovation pipeline has released these ideas, like any other projects in the XYZ Controls Company product and process portfolios they are reviewed for their performance:

Phase 6	IDEA	EVALUATION	TOGGLE
2	Sensor for room occupancy	Developed and sold	Yes
3	Live chat website feature	Not worth it	No
4	Build another factory in Mexico	Study ongoing	Decision in 12 months

After six months, the new occupancy sensors are selling well, but the live chat feature on the website has been deemed superfluous—it turns out the clients of XYZ Controls Company don't need it. The Mexico factory study is still ongoing, with a decision date of no later than twelve months from now.

Was this batch of ideas worth the investment in the process?

Yes! The new room occupancy sensor is adding to the company's revenue stream. The live chat feature didn't cost much to try, and the company learned something about its customers. And the idea of building another factory in Mexico is being closely studied.

The innovation pipeline has a simple philosophical premise: understand our business, our market, our customer, and our organizational vision so well that we know exactly the kinds of innovations we're looking for. When you do that, you can set up an opportunity machine that can automatically screen innovations for their relevancy and move them quickly toward commercialization or deployment.

Too many organizations don't know what they're looking for, making it impossible to filter ideas because they can't recognize a good one. In addition, many organizations look at innovation as a risk management function, and as we've stated before, when you look at it from such a perspective, no really good idea will ever make it through the pipeline.

YOUR ATTITUDE COUNTS!

The vast majority of innovation pipelines are set up and operated in order to *avoid* innovations and *reject them* because they represent *risk*.

It seems crazy, but it's true.

Too many organizations are led by risk-averse people who, despite their squeamishness, are aware they need to appear to welcome new ideas. So they set up an innovation center, or have an innovation day, or install an email employee suggestion box. They're not really interested in the fruits of these efforts. They just want to be able to put a check mark on the list of things that organizations are supposed to do to look good in the eyes of stakeholders, investors, and the public.

This is the truth: your innovation pipeline is not a risk management tool.

It's an opportunity tool.

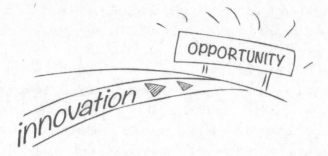

Will it deliver solid-gold nuggets, one after the other, like a goose laying golden eggs?

Absolutely not. As we have seen, 80 percent of the ideas coming into your spark generator will be rejected instantly. Kapow! Gone. Never to be seen again.

And of the 20 percent that pass through the fast filter, only one in ten will be accepted. The other nine will require more study. Of these, perhaps two will eventually be made operational.

So out of a grand total of one hundred ideas that enter the spark generator, perhaps three will become reality.

Does that sound bad? Really?

Think about this:

Of all the sales prospects who enter your sales funnel, how many become paying customers?

Three percent? That's a pretty good ratio, isn't it?

When you advertise a key job opening, do you receive one hundred applications? Two hundred? And how many finalists do you end up with? Three or four?

So what's wrong with a 3 percent success rate in your innovation pipeline?

I'd say it's pretty good!

CRAYOLA'S INNOVATION PIPELINE

Yes, you're reading the headline correctly: we're talking about the iconic manufacturer of children's crayons.

The first Crayola crayons were offered for sale on June 10, 1903. They were made of paraffin wax and a color pigment, and, to keep little fingers clean, each was wrapped in a paper sleeve.

One hundred and fifteen years later, they're still made exactly the same way.

At first glance, you'd think Crayola would be the last place on earth you'd find robust innovation.

You would be mistaken.

In a world of electronic toys and computer-savvy children, Crayola has shown surprising agility and imagination. It has also shown a keen awareness of its core competency. A cookie-cutter approach to innovation might have led the company to sideline its crayon business and plunge headlong into digital electronics for kids making art. But company leaders made a careful study of internal obstacles and enablers to innovation, which suggested simpler, easier, and very successful alternatives. Crayola knew it wasn't very good at electronics, but it had deep intellectual property competencies in chemistry—which is actually how the company had first started in the late nineteenth century.

For example, the Color Wonder Mess-Free Airbrush makes it easy for kids to make airbrush pictures. The airbrush sprays out a fine mist of clear ink that comes to life on special Color Wonder Paper.

Crayola Color Escapes are designed to capitalize on the growing market for adult coloring books. It's a good example of an innovation taking the form of identifying an untapped market (adults) and then developing a product to serve that market that is consistent with the company's core brand image and competencies.

This is not to say that Crayola hasn't established a presence in the digital arena. Crayola has no expertise in the digital space, but DAQRI, a Los Angeles–based provider of augmented reality (AR) services and apps, has plenty. In the innovation pipeline, sources of innovations can be internal or external. The external sources can include partnerships or licensing deals with third parties. Working with the super-innovators at DAQRI, the people at Crayola—the makers of a century-old technology—created the Crayola Color Alive Action Coloring Pages. It's an augmented reality product that uses an app on your tablet to animate your drawing.

Here's how it works:

You give your child a Color Alive coloring book that has line drawings of various characters, such as a dragon and a princess. The child chooses one of the drawings as she normally would—say, a dragon—and then colors it. Then, she takes a tablet into which has been loaded the free Color Alive app. She holds the tablet over the drawing, and the camera in the tablet sees the drawing of the dragon, which the child keeps in view on the screen. The app recognizes and locks in on the drawing, which now has crayon coloring, but the black lines are still visible. The software in the tablet does a computer graphic process whereby your child's colors are added to an animated version of the dragon. On the screen of the tablet there appears an image of your child's dragon, in three dimensions, moving and flapping its wings. Once the animated image has been generated, the child can take the tablet anywhere with her lively customized dragon on the screen.

Jeff Rogers, director of portfolio marketing for Crayola, told *Consumer Goods Technology* magazine, "We have always been very comfortable with creativity; we also knew we had an incredible brand and began to recognize that we could leverage it in more ways. . . . What we needed to think about in terms of innovation was not only applying it to product, but to virtually everything we do."

That's right on target: innovative companies don't just think about product innovation, but about innovation in everything they do.[17.]

Set up your innovation pipeline, ensure that's it's filled to capacity with sparks of innovation, and then rigorously measure your input, output, and process.

Here are some of the elements that you need to be able to check off your list:

1. **An active and engaged innovation champion.**

   This person is responsible for the performance of the innovation pipeline. Just like in any other senior position, this individual must have responsibility, authority, and accountability. He or she must also have the appropriate resources to get the job done.

2. **A robust structure.**

   Formalization promotes stability and reduces uncertainty. The operating rules of the spark generator process should be clear and communicated to all members of the organization, characterized by transparent decision-making accountability, and contain specific performance measures. It also needs to be flexible enough to handle disruptive ideas.

3. **Efficient idea sorting and screening.**

   The organization needs one or more mechanisms to separate good ideas from bad ones, and evaluate ideas by means of both business and feasibility analysis. I'll describe such a system in detail in the pages ahead.

4. **Internal cooperation among functions and departments.**

   A new product or process concept must be able to endure scrutiny from different functional perspectives. This necessitates functional cooperation in the screening and evaluation of new ideas. Close coordination among functions and departments ensures preservation of value for a new concept and facilitates the subsequent development phase.

10

THE INNOVATION BRAND PLAN

Quick: name five organizations that are known for their innovation. They can be large or small, service-oriented, or focused on products. Their particular characteristics don't matter as long as you think of them as being truly innovative.

Good! Now think about the public perception of those organizations. If they're publicly held, think in terms of their stock price and investment outlook. Think about the types of people who work for those companies. Think about the "buzz" that surrounds them in the media.

Does your organization have some of that sizzle? That vibe of excitement and fresh possibilities? That creative energy?

Many CEOs say, "Well, it's great that Apple or Tesla or Trendy Brooklyn, Inc., are known as being innovative. But they're in a different league. We're not like that. Innovation is for people who wear jeans and flannel shirts, and who ride bicycles to work. Not us! We're a meat-and-potatoes company."

These CEOs don't realize there are many ways to innovate how you source, prepare, and market your good ol' meat and potatoes. Your customers need not be aware of any of your internal innovations. All they want is the familiar product, which is what you give them.

Innovation is not the exclusive property of the innovation elitists. It can—and should—happen at any organization in any industry.

THE AMAZING MR. SMITH

We once worked with just such a CEO—a nice man who wore a white shirt and a tie, and whose business, at least in his own mind, was non-innovative and didn't have to be. Mr. Smith, as we'll call him, told us in so many words that innovation wasn't applicable to his company.

A few days earlier, the local newspaper had published an article about his business, which made refractories—specialized heat-resistant materials used in furnaces, reactors, and space rockets. The story related how a storm had flooded the entire block where Smith Refractories was located. Amazingly, within a day, Smith Refractories was back in operation, even though neighboring businesses were still down. We asked Mr. Smith how he did it.

His eyes lit up like a kid at his own birthday party.

"Oh, we had a few tricks up our sleeve!" he said with a smile. "We have pumps that we use to cool the machinery. At dawn the day after the storm I got our engineers together and I told 'em to figure out how to get us operational. I said, 'Just do it!' Within an hour they had modified the pumps to take water *out* of the building. Then we did some electrical work so we could run power to the pumps across the roof rather than through the water on the floor. By four in the afternoon, the factory floor was bone dry, and we were ready to roll!"

"So," we replied, "you innovated! And you, Mr. Smith, led the charge!"

He looked at us. "Well, we don't call it that. We call it just getting the job done. I have a great team!"

Okay—fair enough. If you don't want to use the word *innovation*, then call it whatever you want. As Mr. Smith said, *"Just get the job done."* Don't tell Mr. Smith, but the plain fact is that Smith Refractories had an enviable innovation pipeline, which swiftly captured, evaluated, developed, and deployed a new idea that saved the company.

Oh, and by the way, even though Mr. Smith would never boast about this, his company is known among refractory engineers as being a really great place to work. He gets all the top talent and his employee turnover rate is super low.

Which leads us to the next section.

INVEST IN YOUR BRAND?
OF COURSE YOU DO!

There isn't a successful company anywhere that does not carefully build and maintain its successful brand image. This is why companies spend billions of dollars every year on advertisements, promotions, celebrity endorsements, film tie-ins, social media campaigns, and more, all in an effort to convince consumers that their organization can be depended upon for quality and value and every other positive attribute.

Even Smith Refractories has been known to promote itself, mostly in the person of Mr. Smith, who is very active in the B2B universe of the Chamber of Commerce and industry trade associations. He's no dummy—he knows how to keep the Smith brand top of mind!

Just like quality and value, innovation should be a key part of your brand. And not as an empty slogan, but as something the organization lives every day and is willing to invest in.

There are three facets to your innovation brand.

1. Your Current Employees

The people who work at Smith Refractories love their jobs! We know this because of what we've read on websites including Glassdoor, where Smith employees give the company five stars. Remember, with the advent of the internet, employees have a *voice*. They can, and will, broadcast to the world how they *feel* about their jobs. Sadly, some CEOs dismiss these expressions as being from employees who are "disgruntled." They think that because they pay well, nothing else should matter.

Nothing could be further from the truth.

As an employer, you have a choice. You can employ people who are either:

1. *Working just for the paycheck.* They clock in every day, do their jobs as directed, don't make waves, don't go the extra mile because there's no reason to, and clock out at the end of the day. If a better opportunity comes along, in the blink of an eye they'll jump ship. Trust? It's not in their vocabulary.

2. *Working because they love what they do—and getting paid well is the icing on the cake.* They enjoy being challenged, and look forward to collaborating with others, both on the team and in other areas of the organization. When a crisis comes—like the flood that struck Smith Refractories—they're ready to leap into action and get the business back on track. And perhaps most importantly, they're eager to contribute their own new ideas to the company for the common good.

They're willing to go the extra mile because they trust each other and their bosses.

We once worked with a company that faced a crisis during the Great Recession. They were in the housing sector, which was hit hard. When the customer base dried up, the CEO went to her people and said, "We're going to make it. We're not going to lay off a single person. We'll have to take pay cuts, but no one is getting laid off. We're going to find ways of making money in this horrible economy."

And sure enough, she and her team innovated in the face of disaster. They tossed out their old business plan and looked at the market with new eyes. They solicited ideas from every employee and fed the ideas into their innovation pipeline. The economy recovered and the company rebounded, with every employee still on board.

2. The People You Want to Hire

Go back to category #1, your current employees, and the question of which of two types of employees you'd rather have: the clock-punchers or the innovators.

The same goes for your brand among the pool of people who might apply for a job at your company.

When you post a job opening, do you want to attract the attention of the best and the brightest, or those at the bottom of the labor barrel?

Hopefully, the answer is obvious: the best candidates want to work at an organization that's collaborative and innovative, and embraces new ideas while still committed to sound business practices.

As Neil Blumenthal, co-founder and CEO of Warby Parker, said on Business.com, "The first thing is you have to hire the right people, and the question is, how do you hire the right people? . . . We're looking for certain characteristics that allow for innovation."[1]

There's a saying going around now: "All the talented people have great jobs!" At the time of this writing, unemployment is low, and there are few qualified people who are out of work. But there are plenty of highly qualified people who are unhappy in their current roles! They feel stifled, or unappreciated, or stuck with no path ahead. They are open to making a change. As a leader, you need to ask yourself two questions:

1. "Are the people at my company unhappy and ready to jump ship to one of my competitors?" If the answer is yes, you need to correct this problem. You need to upgrade the *employee experience* at your organization. I'm not just talking about how much you pay them or if you offer free coffee and bagels in the break room. I'm talking about how you engage their minds and stimulate their imaginations. How you can help give *meaning* to their work.

2. "Is our company capable of stealing the very best from our competitors?" If the answer is no, you need to correct this problem. See "1" above.

3. The Outside World: Customers, Partners, Investors

Customers want to *feel good* about the products and services they buy from you.

Your partners—suppliers, licensors, strategic alliances—want to *feel good* about doing business with you.

And, of course, your investors want to *feel super good* about where they've parked their money.

These constituencies all have choices. The world is a big place, and becoming more interconnected every day. Products are made all over the world and shipped to consumers thousands of miles away. Money flows around the world too. Just a few decades ago, even global businesses were more regional.

For example, the Ford Motor Company, which for decades was synonymous with Detroit, operates factories in nations around the world including Thailand, Portugal, Brazil, France, China, Mexico, South Africa, and more.

Meanwhile, foreign automakers with plants in the United States include Toyota, Honda, Nissan, Mazda, Subaru, Hyundai, Kia, Volkswagen, Volvo, BMW, Daimler AG, and Hino Motors.

Competition for investment dollars and strategic partnerships is fierce! And thanks to innovations in finance, it's getting easier for ordinary "mom and pop" investors to put their money in innovative companies. Platforms like Kickstarter and Indiegogo are seeing increasing success. From its inception in 2009 to 2018—only nine years—Kickstarter saw more than $3.9 billion pledged to projects from everyday people. Indiegogo has championed the launch of many futuristic projects, including the world's smallest camera and smart nano drones.[2]

Meanwhile, federal regulations surrounding initial public offerings (IPOs) are loosening. In 2015, the US Securities and Exchange Commission (SEC) finalized the rules under JOBS Act Title IV (commonly known as Regulation A+), which provides nonaccredited investors with the opportunity to invest in emerging companies, with certain limitations.

In the past, the opportunity to invest in IPOs was reserved for the big institutional investors and wealthy clients of investment banks. But the playing field for all investors is being leveled by changes in the way the financial industry has traditionally operated, not unlike how Uber disrupted the transportation industry.

Is your company positioned to take advantage of the tremendous public interest in companies that innovate, or do you want to stand on the sidelines while the world passes you by?

INNOVATION = PUTTING YOUR PANTS ON EVERY MORNING

You probably already innovate in ways you don't even think about. You just need to *focus* on it and *invest* in it.

The Innovation Mandate is not the property of the "innovation elite" or something to be held in a secret black box.

Innovation works best when it's something you do without thinking about, like getting dressed in the morning.

It's got to have a natural flow, like a familiar song at a steady tempo.

In fact, one problem many companies face is *innovation overexuberance*.

Huh?

This happens when well-meaning leaders jump on the innovation bandwagon and then declare "mission accomplished" long before the results are in.

Here's how the sad story could unfold at a company we'll call Apex Industries.

The leader will fall under the spell of a consultant (never a good thing!) and become convinced that "this innovation thing" is the way to go. A skeletal version of an innovation operating system is hastily set up and an innovation pipeline designated. Big announcements are made that Apex Industries is committed to being an innovation leader. This is nothing more than a branding effort designed to appeal to the investors. The whole thing looks like a house of cards.

Under the newly minted Apex Industries innovation system, one or two interesting ideas will somehow squeeze past the toggle manager whose real job is to find ways to kill innovative ideas because they're risky. The ideas that emerge are starving little orphans that have no support from the rest of the organization. If a new product is introduced, there's no perfect plan. There's no marketing campaign, or the supply chain is weak, or the quality control is missing. Exuberance quickly turns to cynicism as employees see through the expensive charade.

The result for Apex is loss of market leadership, declining profits, and eventual death by sale or bankruptcy.

At a big company, it's easy to create and fund an innovation center or skunkworks—and by doing so hold innovation at arm's length. Your chosen innovators may come up with some really interesting and radical ideas, but unless you have a robust innovation operating system to capture and exploit these breakthroughs, you'll be both wasting your time and money, and fanning the flames of cynicism among your employees.

Too often the scheme is never supported by a strategic plan backed up by resources, and as soon as some crisis arises, such as an economic turndown, the whole idea is shelved.

Innovation is no different from any other operating system. It needs to be a familiar part of the organization, and connected securely to every department, office, cubicle, and employee. The innovation pipeline needs to be full to capacity on every day of the calendar. Those new ideas represent money in the bank—if not today then tomorrow—as well as make the organization a more attractive place to work.

Would you walk out of the house in the morning without getting dressed? I'll bet you wouldn't. It's something you do because that's the way the world works.

Would you try to run a business that had made a conscious decision to *not innovate*? Probably not!

WHO ARE YOUR INNOVATION SUPERSTARS?

Innovation is a people-powered process.

After all, new ideas don't come from computers (at least not yet!).

It takes a human being to look at a problem or situation and say, "I think we could do this better."

It's the average employee who says:

"We could make our customer experience better if we _____."

"We could improve the quality of our product if we _____."

"We could enhance employee productivity if we _____."

"We could reduce *muda*—waste—in our production process if we _____."

To *connect* with your employees and stakeholders, you need to articulate to them what innovation means to your company, how they can each contribute, and how you're going to support it.

Make it clear you're looking for innovation superstars, and they can come from any department.

If your custodian comes up with a way to clean the floors that saves the company time and money, then your custodian might be an innovation superstar.

How about leveraging the superstar innovative spark of the crowd? Industrial giant GE is doing just that with its crowdsourcing platform GE Fuse. In 2016, GE launched Fuse as an open crowdsourcing platform connected to a network of "microfactories" capable of rapid design and prototyping. As part of GE's GeniusLink, a team that works with experts inside and outside of GE to find more efficient ways to do business, Fuse created a new forum where people from all over the world participate in a multitude of technical challenges. "This will be an ongoing robust business operation," said GeniusLink director and Fuse president Dyan Finkhousen. "For us, it's about matching great talent and great solutions with great need."[3]

According to the Deloitte Millennial Survey 2014, when millennials look for a job, 78 percent want to work for a company that encourages innovation and creative thinking, and most say their current employer doesn't provide this. In fact, they believe the top two barriers to innovation are "management attitude" (63 percent) and "operational structures and procedures" (61 percent).[4]

No matter where you find them—in the lab, the janitorial closet, the crowd, or your delivery trucks—innovation superstars are all around you. All you have to do is capture their sparks and turn them into value for your company and your customers!

SELF-DRIVING PUBLIC TRANSIT IN DETROIT

It's only fitting that the streets of Detroit, historically America's capital of the motor vehicle industry, may soon be filled with innovative, self-driving, publicly accessible vehicles.

At least that's the mission of May Mobility, an Ann Arbor, Michigan–based startup, which is developing an urban micro-transit service using six-passenger electric vehicles that steer themselves through traffic on a carefully mapped, closed loop. On June 26, 2018, its first commercial deployment began with a fleet of friendly green-and-white shuttles, each with a top speed of twenty-five miles per hour, displacing those big diesel buses on at least one mile-long Bedrock route.[5]

For now, each vehicle still has a human in the front seat to take control if necessary. Eventually the shuttles will operate totally on their own.

The company has announced plans to expand to Columbus, Ohio, and add another route in Grand Rapids, Michigan. It's a rapid acceleration for a company that was founded in 2016. But the innovation leaders at the helm have brought deep experience to the project. CEO and co-founder Edwin Olson acted as lead investigator on Ford's autonomous driving program, and was also a co-director focused on autonomous driving at Toyota Research Institute. Co-founder and COO Alisyn Malek previously worked at GM Ventures, where she oversaw the relationship with then-startup Cruise Automation, which was subsequently acquired by GM and brought in-house to help develop that automaker's internal self-driving technology.[6]

Innovation often requires collaboration, both in brainpower and cash. May Mobility raised $11.5 million in seed funding in 2018 from BMW i VENTURES, Toyota AI, and others. Trucks, Maven Ventures, and Tandem Ventures are also investors in the company.

The leaders of May Mobility stress that this is no academic exercise. The goal of the company is to get vehicles on the road, carrying real passengers, as quickly as possible. The plan is to set modest goals and meet them, all the while learning how to do better. The innovations won't stop just because the system is working; for May Mobility, having real-world vehicles on the street is a vital part of the innovation process. As Olson said, "We think that by getting out in to the real world we can not only build a successful business, but we can turn on a flow of data and operational know-how that will help us move and improve our systems faster than the original equipment manufacturers which are in research and development mode."[7]

1. **Establish your innovation brand.**

   I'll bet you're careful about the image of your brand in the market-place. You want to stand for quality, value, and a great customer experience. Make sure you're just as dedicated to your innovation brand! Be known as the place where great ideas originate. It's like putting money in the bank.

2. **Cultivate employee innovation.**

   How do you encourage your employees to be engaged and willing to go the extra mile for the organization? Not by treating them like cogs in a wheel, but by cultivating their natural desire to solve problems and find new solutions.

3. **Make sure your company attracts the top performers.**

   The competition for the best employees is fierce and increasingly global. A good candidate for a key position in your company may be weighing multiple job offers from across the street or from another continent. By positioning your organization as an innovation leader, in the battle for top talent you'll help tip the scales in your favor.

4. **Keep your investors happy.**

   When the next Warren Buffett is scanning the investment landscape looking for a company that shows value, he or she doesn't want to see lackluster performance and a ho-hum attitude toward innovation. They're looking for dynamism and growth, and those are fueled by just one thing: a steady and predictable stream of new ideas. Keep your company on the A list for investors by showing them your commitment to innovation.

LONG-TERM INNOVATION SUCCESS

How long has your organization been in business?

If you're Kongō Gumi Co., Ltd., the Japanese construction company specializing in Buddhist temples, you've been in continuous operation since it was founded in the year 578 CE. That's right, we're not missing a few centuries; the company operated independently for over 1,400 years, until it was absorbed as a subsidiary of Takamatsu in 2006.

Imagine that!

In the United States, one of the oldest continuously operating companies is Caswell-Massey, founded in 1752. It's the oldest American consumer brand in operation.[1]

Do you think their way of doing business has changed in over 250 years? You bet it has! Would the folks at Caswell-Massey claim to be "innovators"? I'll let you decide. Here's a quote from the company website (which, by the way, is a pretty good website) under the headline "Our Future": "As we approach nearly three centuries of being an American Original, we plan to bring out the best from our archives, strengthen our community of loyal customers, and create incredible new products and collaborations worthy of a legendary American brand."

Creating "incredible new products and collaborations" sounds a lot like innovation to me.

The spark of innovation is burning bright at this venerable brand!

You probably haven't been around as long as Kongō Gumi or Caswell-Massey. Your company may be comfortably ensconced in middle age or fresh out of the startup gate. You may be stuck in a rut and looking for a new shot of inspiration (if so, you've come to the right place!), or you want to be sure your new venture is positioned for success.

Either way, you need to make innovation an integral part of what you do every day to satisfy your customers.

TAKE A DEEP BREATH . . . AND START!

If you look at organizations around the world, you'll see that no two innovation operating systems are exactly the same. That's actually a good thing, because your brand of innovation begins with building your customized innovation operating system. There should be a foundational infrastructure based on what works for the most organizations, which then *must* be customized to fit your goals in the beautiful uniqueness that is your enterprise.

You've made it this far in the book. Congratulations! But the time for book learning is drawing to a close. It's time to take action.

"Where do I start?" you ask.

Read on!

1. Know and Serve Your Customer

The first fundamental question you need to answer is, "Who is my customer, and what do they need from us?"

To answer this, start with the super-obvious facts that may seem boring but are necessary to understand as you build a rock-solid foundation to your innovation operating system.

Start at the *very beginning*.

The world's industries can be roughly divided into three groups, each with its own industrial sectors. Your organization is in one of these three groups:

1. **Product providers.** Examples include Nike (sportswear), Tesla (cars), Domino's Pizza (food), Lego (toys), Proctor & Gamble (personal products), Samsung (electronics). These companies make things that they sell to you. Their priority will be on new product innovations.

2. **Service providers.** Marriott International (hotels), Uber (transportation), H&R Block (tax prep), Amazon (retail sales), Angie's List (business ratings), Sprint (phone), LinkedIn (business networking), US Postal Service (snail mail). Because they don't make products, their priority will be on service innovations.

3. **A combination of both.** The US Army (provides services and produces its own products with contractors), Apple (builds computers and also provides services like iTunes streaming), McDonald's (produces food, but service is a core selling proposition), Ascension Health (the largest nonprofit hospital system in the United States, with massive inventory and infrastructure investments).

Obviously these categories are fluid, and every company has exposure to some combination of products and services. What matters to your innovation operating system is what you judge to be the normally expected mix of new ideas and how they need to be processed. A company such as Ford, with its massive assembly lines and complex supply chain, has an innovation operating system that in its appearance and function is very different from that of Uber. Yours will be different from theirs, and from any other company's.

The point is, what does *your* organization provide to your customers? What do they buy from you that they can't get anywhere else?

Do your customers expect you to produce dazzling new gadgets every year? Or do they experience your company primarily through the services you offer, like when you check into a hotel or perform a search on Google?

Your innovation operating system must be geared toward the prime directive. It needs to seek out, identify, and operationalize innovations.

And—just as a friendly reminder—innovation is:

**The creation of new value that serves your
organization's mission and customer.**

Some companies, such as ABC Medical Device Company, introduced earlier
in this book, and which produces specialized products for a niche market, may
have a tightly defined innovation pipeline. But to be accurate, the ABC Medical
Device pipeline is really a *new product pipeline*, not unlike the pipelines that pharmaceutical companies have. It's designed specifically to process new inventions
that may or may not prove suitable for its product line. What the leaders of ABC
Medical Device need to remember is that innovation must also find a home in
the company's *internal processes*.

EVERYTHING YOU DO AFFECTS YOUR CUSTOMER

For example, let's say that ABC Medical Device succeeds in attracting the most
innovative and cutting-edge tools for its product line; and in terms of what the
customer sees as the product line, it's the leader in its market.

But then let's hypothesize that, operationally, ABC Medical Device:

- Pays its employees with paper checks—no direct deposit is available.
- Uses an outdated company intranet with no system of real-time
  dashboards providing timely key performance indicators.
- Experiences persistent downtime on its production lines due to poor
  quality control of incoming parts.
- Misplaces inventory due to lack of investment in basic inventory
  management software and radio frequency identification (RFID) tags.
- Has been sued by female employees who allege workplace harassment.

So despite having an enviable product innovation pipeline, ABC Medical Device
may be *losing money* because it has failed to innovate in key areas of its operations!

Everything you do affects the value you bring to your customer. Customers are
totally self-centered. They are not charitable organizations. Their loyalty to your
brand is not set in stone. The moment you slip or your brand is tarnished, they
will abandon you and flock to whoever offers the best value.

This is why innovation needs to be baked into every molecule of your organization. Innovation does not just mean producing shiny new products. It means behaving rationally and recognizing that **standing still = falling behind = failure.**

2. Perform a Self-Assessment

In business, knowledge of your own company is mandatory for long-term success. Therefore, regular organizational self-assessments need to be a vital part of your everyday operations. You should:

- Regularly perform SWOT analyses, know your organization's strengths and weaknesses, and identify opportunities and threats.
- Have a good sense of your long-term growth strategy and how you intend to maintain domination of your market.
- Be realistic about your people and their attitude toward innovation, or more broadly, their level of engagement with each other, their managers, and the mission of the company.

If any of this seems foreign to you, please immediately close this book and either begin to plan a program of self-assessment or hire a reputable consultant who can guide you through the process. There's no point in thinking about innovation unless you've got the basic tools in place.

Okay? Let's proceed.

IS THERE A COMPANY CULTURE OF INNOVATION?

The first thing you need to figure out is whether your company culture has a tradition of innovation.

This question is not as easy as you might think.

Consider the example of the Xerox PARC division. Founded in 1970 as a division of Xerox Corporation, the Palo Alto Research Center is a research and development company in Palo Alto, California, with a solid reputation for its contributions to information technology and hardware systems. PARC was founded precisely because of a self-assessment spearheaded by Charles McColough, Xerox's co-founder who was then serving as CEO. He recognized that because Xerox's existing research staff was focused on making copiers more efficiently and with incrementally better features, they were not likely to be adept in innovating the new, breakthrough technology of personal computing. That's why he established PARC as an independent unit located on the opposite side of the country as Xerox's headquarters in Rochester, New York. He hired top talent, funded the operation, and sent them to work tackling big problems.

They produced amazing innovations, including the graphical user interface (GUI), computer mouse, Ethernet, laser printing, and simple WYSIWYG (what you see is what you get) word processing software. They put them all together in the Alto personal computer, which Xerox introduced to the market in 1973.

The innovators at PARC were truly years ahead of their time. So what happened? Why is Apple the personal computer leader and not Xerox?

Because just as PARC was producing exciting new innovations, Xerox was facing intense market pressure from competitors including Canon and Ricoh. Company leaders in Rochester needed quick growth to satisfy investors, so they ordered the Alto to be rushed to market. As Maxwell Wessel wrote for *Harvard Business Review*, "But instead of determining the right customer base and sales techniques through thoughtful experimentation, management decided to push the PC through its existing sales channel. It was the fastest way to turn potential dollars into real ones, after all. Discovery had been abandoned; delivery was the new mantra."[2]

Sales were poor because Xerox salespeople weren't properly prepared to advocate for this new product, which was totally unlike an office copier and was best suited for the mass market. Xerox wasn't nimble enough to transition to a brand-new market with which it had no experience.

In 1979, Steve Jobs made his now legendary visit to the PARC lab and came away amazed. He and Apple engineers promptly reworked the Lisa computer with many of the features found on the Alto, with the big exception that Apple made the product profitable in the mass market. For example, the mouse that the PARC engineers designed cost three hundred dollars to build and wasn't durable. It was intended for the high-end corporate user. The mouse that Jobs created for the Macintosh cost less than fifteen dollars to build and was much more functional for an everyday user.[3]

As Thomas Alva Edison wrote a century ago, "There is a wide difference between completing an invention and putting the manufactured article on the market." He would know—like Steve Jobs, Edison was a master at both.

Your self-assessment needs to cover all the bases. Here's a quick survey that will give you an idea of where you stand and what areas you need to improve as you begin to leverage the amazing power of innovation. Normally this type of Likert scale would have five levels of response, but to make it easy we're going to give you just three.

STATEMENT	RESPONSES		
	NO	I DON'T KNOW	YES
We have a clear organizational mission.			
We know who our customers are and what they need from us.			
Our leadership team embraces innovation.			
Our employees embrace innovation.			
Our employees are ready to trust leadership with their new ideas.			
We've identified functional areas that can especially benefit from innovation.			
We know how innovation can help us either add value or cut expense—both are good outcomes.			
We have the necessary financial resources to follow through on good new ideas.			
We have the necessary cross-functional relationships between employees and teams to make a new idea work.			
We have identified an innovation champion— individual or team.			
We're ready to set up our innovation operating system and innovation pipeline.			
We can take ideas and turn them into value for our customers.			

As you can see, there's no scoring on this survey. There's no "winning" or "losing." This is a tool for you to gauge your leadership and organizational readiness to innovate. And you'll see that "I don't know" is a perfectly legitimate response . . . and one that might be the choice of most leaders to most of the statements.

3. Identify and Empower an Innovation Champion

At every company, someone—a real human being—needs to have the responsibility and authority to oversee the innovation operating system and its key component, the innovation pipeline.

At a small company, it could be the CEO or owner.

At a medium-sized company, it could be a team or committee of managers, with a ranking member.

At a big company, it could be an individual officer supported by staff.

These people must be responsible for:

Planning

1. Allocating resources and setting up teams, with the eye on long-term capability
2. Determining and deploying the automated toggle settings for each phase of the innovation pipeline

Building

1. Managing the innovation operating system and monitoring the progress of the various ongoing initiatives
2. Building out innovation capabilities and embedding them within the corporate culture to impact the broader organization

Operating

1. Evaluating ideas that either pass through the automated toggles or fall outside the automated system. This includes employee suggestions, ideas for partnerships or licensing, and unexpected or unplanned product ideas.
2. Performing or causing to be performed the necessary due diligence to determine if an idea is worthy of further study or even immediate approval
3. Follow-through to ensure that approved innovations don't fall through the cracks, get buried, or vanish into the company bureaucracy
4. Communication with relevant stakeholders, including the person or team who submitted the idea, the people whose jobs it may impact, and the person who approves funding

Reviewing

1. Periodic (quarterly or annual) evaluation of the return on investment of the innovation operating system, as best as can be ascertained. Product innovations are easy to evaluate because, once they're launched, they're

tracked like any other product for profitability. Process innovations can be evaluated by using the relevant key performance metrics.

BY ANY OTHER NAME . . .

While we think the title "innovation champion" is perfect, you can call this person anything you want. Other titles may include head of innovation, innovation director, and chief innovation officer. Titles with a narrower scope include innovation product manager, innovation project manager, and new business developer.

Sometimes confused with the innovation champion is the head of R&D. While concerned with innovation, "R&D" suggests a focus that's purely on new product development, which is narrow and may not even be a significant part of your company. And your innovation champion needs to oversee the big picture and complement the purely technological advancements with capabilities to build the new products and business cases that support their deployment.

4. Create Your Innovation Mandate

Here's a simple pre-flight Innovation Mandate checklist. As any pilot knows, the pre-flight checklist is critical. Not only must you go through it *before* deployment, as you embed your Innovation Mandate into every corner and cubicle of your company, but you should review it periodically to ensure your innovation machine is running smoothly and with optimum output.

This is your checklist of the elements of your Innovation Mandate:

- √ The vision
- √ The mission
- √ Thoughtful team architecture
- √ A robust innovation pipeline
- √ A well-defined brand and communication plan
- √ A formal project management infrastructure
- √ Executive dashboards to report out across multifunctional teams
- √ Ongoing and regular ideation and innovation activities
- √ Regularly scheduled success reporting
- √ An internal innovation software package for collaboration that leverages game mechanics and social engagement

√ An internal customer experience strategy
√ Verifiable results
√ Proven return on innovation investment
√ Happy stakeholders and customers!

5. Review, Review, and Review Again

The number one problem with many innovation efforts is that they're set up, they sputter to life, they produce a few good ideas, the champagne corks fly and backs are slapped in congratulations, and then the whole silly experiment is forgotten and it's back to business as usual.

Ironically, this pattern is followed by the same hard-nosed executives who:

• carefully track the performance over time of a key product in the marketplace;
• give detailed employee performance reviews every year, and believe they're useful (they aren't);
• check their 401(k) accounts every morning at breakfast;
• demand an ROI report for everything the company spends money on; and
• watch the company's stock price as it goes up and down.

They're used to tracking performance over time of things that are important to them, but for some reason—perhaps because they think that innovation is something magical and uncontrollable—they don't do the same with innovation.

If you take just one idea from this book, it must be this:

> **Innovation is not magic. It can be managed and**
> **planned like any other part of your operations.**

This means plan, execute, review, adjust, and execute again. Just as a sports team or athlete trains. Every time you go through the cycle, you get a little bit better. The sparks start flying faster. The blaze of innovation burns a little bit hotter.

EXAMPLE: EVALUATING A SUPPLY CHAIN INNOVATION

Let's go back to ABC Medical Device Company. After suffering sustained declining revenues, company leaders saw the light, embraced the Innovation Mandate, and built an innovation operating system. One of the first ideas to be implemented was the deployment of RFID devices to track inventory at every stage of the supply chain.

The anticipated value of RFID tagging of products and pallets included:

- RFID tags can hold much larger amounts and different types of data than traditional bar codes.
- RFID does not require direct line of sight for scanning. The product or case that's been tagged can be anywhere, even at the bottom of the pile, and it will be tracked.
- RFID provides real-time updates and faster scanning. There's zero time lag. If a truck is running late, the inventory manager knows this even before the guys on the loading dock who are waiting for it.
- RFID can reduce labor costs. Manual tracking required multiple employees; with RFID, one inventory manager can track thousands of items.
- RFID tracks returnable empty containers, which have a habit of disappearing.

The biggest negative for RFID is the cost. But will the savings in time and money make up for it?

After a year of full deployment in the ABC Medical Device supply chain, analysis determined that the RFID system was showing a good ROI on shipping containers, very time-sensitive shipments, and expensive finished goods. In these applications, they produced measurable savings.

The RFID system was judged to have a poor return on investment on the routine shipping of lower-priced finished goods, except at the level of the shipping container or truck. Bar codes were just as effective and at a much lower cost.

The innovation was judged an overall success because it proved to be a new idea or process that helped the organization fulfill its mission—and at a profit. But after the review it was fine-tuned and the applications where it didn't make a difference or add value were discontinued.

Remember, just because something is new doesn't mean you have to accept it.

You should investigate it and determine its utility. If it looks useful, try it. If it doesn't, then don't.

Another new idea is coming around the corner!

THE INNOVATION LEADER YOU'VE PROBABLY NEVER HEARD OF

Not every innovation leader is a household name like Apple, Amazon, or Google.

On the *Forbes* magazine list of "World's Most Innovative Companies 2018," the top spot was claimed by a company named ServiceNow.[4]

Who?

Founded in 2004 and based in Santa Clara, California, ServiceNow, Inc., provides cloud-based services to automate enterprise information technology operations. In plain English, the company provides a simple, flexible workflow that allows employees to easily manage their requests from the information technology (IT) department—everything from getting a new phone to health-care plan information. It's a rich market, dominated (until now) by big companies including BMC Software, Hewlett Packard Enterprise, Cherwell Software, and CA Technologies.

Why is it the leader?

"ServiceNow's innovation lies in its elegance," explained the CEO of Acorio, Ellen Daley, a former member of the executive team at Forrester Research. "It's solving a common but complex problem—processes and assignment of work—with a cloud-native, holistic approach that is easy to maintain and use."[5] The company's attitude is this: If a teenager can reset their Instagram password in fifteen seconds, why must an employee who wants to reset their work email have to wait twenty minutes and make a phone call to the guy in information technology?

The founder and CEO is Fred Luddy. In 2004, he was pretty much broke, having seen a personal fortune of $35 million vanish overnight in the midst of accounting fraud at his previous company, Peregrine Systems. (He was not involved in any misdeeds.) "I really hated my job," Luddy told *Forbes*. "Losing that money was absolutely the best thing that could have happened."[6]

He became a one-man shop, tinkering with ServiceNow's core product from his home. In July 2005, ServiceNow raised its first funds, a $2.5 million Series A round led by JMI Equity. From that point, its growth was rapid, signing up customers including Deutsche Bank, Intel, and McDonald's, and reaching one hundred employees.

At that point, Luddy knew he needed a CEO who could manage growth. In 2011, with a level of humility rare in the corner office, he transitioned from CEO to chief product officer.

Like true innovators, ServiceNow demands that innovation produce practical results. "This is not technology in service of technology," said current CEO John Donahoe. "We want to enhance the quality of the lives of people at work, whether you're an IT help-desk professional or an end user."[7]

Isn't that the bottom line: to enhance the quality of life?

1. **Know and serve your customer.**

    Everything you do must be focused on bringing more value to your customer—and, to do that, you need a steady flow of new ideas.

2. **Perform a self-assessment.**

    Take an honest look at yourself, your people, and your organization, and judge how prepared you are to ramp up your innovation pipeline.

3. **Identify and empower an innovation champion.**

    The buck must stop at someone's desk. Innovation is a people-powered activity, and you need people to take responsibility for it.

4. **Plan, build, and deploy your innovation operating system.**

    Innovation is the transformation of ideas into reality. Start by taking your idea of an innovation operating system and making it real.

5. **Review, review, and review again.**

    Persistence is the key to success. Innovation is a numbers game—there will be many sparks, but few will ignite. That's okay!

PARTING THOUGHTS

THE INNOVATION MANDATE TOP TEN LIST

Thank you for reading this book! It's delivered a lot of information, and no doubt you'll take the parts you need and use them to create your Innovation Mandate, capture the sparks of innovation, and turn them into profits.

Before we go, here's a handy top ten list of things you absolutely must understand and put into action. If you can check off every one of these, you'll be well on your way to becoming an innovation superstar.

Here they are:

THE INNOVATION MANDATE TOP TEN LIST

1. Know why your organization needs to innovate.
2. Be personally ready to innovate, and ensure your people are ready and willing.
3. Identify areas you could target for innovation.
4. Formulate your innovation mission.
5. Appoint an innovation champion or team.
6. Build your innovation operating system.
7. Create your innovation pipeline.
8. Provide adequate funding and resources.
9. Sustain the effort over time and in every area of your organization.
10. Review and evaluate the results on a regular basis.

Over the course of thousands of years of human history, we've made our lives better by figuring out new ways to perform work, enjoy life, manage our institutions, and save lives. The process of turning new ideas into reality has always been, and still is, the cornerstone of progress.

Only humans have the spark of innovation. It's at the very core of who we are. It makes life interesting and fun. It helps each generation live better than the previous one.

From a business perspective, innovation—in all its many forms—is the key to profits. If you stay the same, you fall behind. The only way to keep moving forward and keep the profits coming is to innovate.

Thank you for reading this book. Now go and start working on your next innovation!

NOTES

Introduction
1. Ilan Mochari, "Why Half of the S&P 500 Companies Will Be Replaced in the Next Decade," *Inc.*, March 23, 2016, https://www.inc.com/ilan-mochari /innosight-sp-500-new-companies.html.
2. Dylan Minor, Paul Brook, and Josh Bernoff, "Are Innovative Companies Profitable?" *MIT Sloan Management Review*, December 28, 2017, https://sloan review.mit.edu/article/are-innovative-companies-more-profitable/.
3. "100 Fastest-Growing Companies," *Fortune*, http://fortune.com/100-fastest -growing-companies/.

Chapter 1: Those Little Sparks Are Worth Money!
1. "Fortune 1000 Executives' Perspectives on Enterprise Innovation," Olympus America, October 14, 2010, http://www.olympusamerica.com/corporate/docs /EnterpriseInnovationExecOmnisurvey.pdf?intCmp=corp_rdir_Innovation ExecOmnisurvey.
2. Dylan Minor, Paul Brook, and Josh Bernoff, "Are Innovative Companies Profitable?" *MIT Sloan Management Review*, https://sloanreview.mit.edu/article /are-innovative-companies-more-profitable/.
3. "Video: Steve Jobs's Commencement speech at Stanford University," Gurteen, http://www.gurteen.com/gurteen/gurteen.nsf/id/ding-in-universe.
4. "User-Driven Innovation," Dewalt, https://www.dewalt.com/dewalt-dna /innovation-technology.
5. "Successful Trial Integration of DHL Parcelcopter into Logistics Chain," DHL, May 9, 2016, http://www.dhl.com/en/press/releases/releases_2016/all/parcel _ecommerce/successful_trial_integration_dhl_parcelcopter_logistics_chain.html.
6. "Material Handling Focus: Pressure grows in the e-com last mile," *Logistics Middle East*, May 28, 2018, https://www.logisticsmiddleeast.com/warehouse/30814 -material-handling-focus-pressure-grows-in-the-e-com-last-mile.
7. "Staff Suggestion Scheme success British Airways' £20 mn savings," Vetter, https://www.getvetter.com/casestudies/britishairwaysstaffsuggestionscheme.
8. Barbara Speed, "'A cursed project': a short history of the Facebook 'like' button," *New Statesman America*, October 9, 2015, https://www.newstatesman.com /science-tech/social-media/2015/10/cursed-project-short-history-facebook-button.

9. "Cassidy Goldstein," Lemelson-MIT, http://lemelson.mit.edu/resources/cassidy
-goldstein.

10. Regina Hope Sinsky, "84-year-old becomes oldest app inventor with the word
game Dabble," Venture Beat, August 17, 2011, https://venturebeat.com/2011
/08/17/84-year-old-becomes-eldest-app-inventor-with-a-word-game-called
-dabble/.

11. Ira Kalb, "Is Apple Becoming More Like Toyota in Its Approach to Innovation?"
Huffington Post, January 26, 2017, https://www.huffingtonpost.com
/ira-kalb/is-apple-becoming-more-li_b_9085164.html.

12. Larry Keeley, *Ten Types of Innovation: The Discipline of Building Breakthroughs*
(Hoboken, N.J.: Wiley, 2013).

13. Stephen Williams, "Paddle shifters move from the fast track to the commuter lane,"
New York Times News Service, July 14, 2017, https://www.boston.com/cars
/car-news/2017/07/14/paddle-shifters-move-from-the-fast-track-to-the-commuter
-lane.

14. Stephen Williams, "Paddle shifters move from the fast track to the commuter lane."

15. Thomas A. Stewart and Anand P. Raman, "Lessons from Toyota's Long Drive,"
Harvard Business Review, July–August 2007, https://hbr.org/2007/07
/lessons-from-toyotas-long-drive.

16. Jessica Hullinger, "18 Secrets of UPS Drivers," *Mental Floss*, December 11, 2015,
http://mentalfloss.com/article/60556/18-secrets-ups-drivers.

17. Cailey Rizzo, "UPS Trucks Don't Turn Left and Neither Should You (Video),"
Travel and Leisure, February 6, 2017, https://www.travelandleisure.com
/travel-tips/ground-transportation/why-ups-trucks-dont-turn-left.

18. Jessica Hullinger, "18 Secrets of UPS Drivers."

19. "Face ID," Wikipedia, last edited April 3, 2019, 14:21, https://en.wikipedia
.org/wiki/Face_ID.

20. "Here's A List Of 57 Bankruptcies In The Retail Apocalypse And Why They
Failed," CB Insights, October 17, 2018, https://www.cbinsights.com/research
/retail-apocalypse-timeline-infographic/.

21. Rick Mullin, "Tufts Study Finds Big Rise In Cost Of Drug Development,"
Chemical & Engineering News, November 20, 2014, https://cen.acs.org/articles
/92/web/2014/11/Tufts-Study-Finds-Big-Rise.html.

22. Loren Grush, "SpaceX makes aerospace history with successful launch and landing
of a used rocket," *The Verge*, March 30, 2017, https://www.theverge.com
/2017/3/30/15117096/spacex-launch-reusable-rocket-success-falcon-9-landing.

23. Brad Power, "How Toyota Pulls Improvement from the Front Line," *Harvard
Business Review*, June 24, 2011, https://hbr.org/2011/06/how-toyota-pulls
-improvement-f.

24. "Who Invented Sticky Notes?" Post-It Brand, Thursday, April 4, 2013,
https://www.post-it.com/3M/en_US/post-it/contact-us/about-us/.

25. Leigh Ann Anderson, ed., "Viagra: How a Little Blue Pill Changed the World,"
Drugs.com, February 12, 2018, https://www.drugs.com/slideshow/viagra-little
-blue-pill-1043.

26. Alex Pedrosa, "Motivating Stakeholders for Co-created Innovation," *Technology Innovation Management Review*, December 2009, https://timreview.ca/article/311.
27. "Supplier Base Management: Managing the Whole, Not Just the Parts," 95th Annual International Supply Management Conference, May 2010, https://www.instituteforsupplymanagement.org/files/Pubs/Proceedings/2010ProcEC-Melnyk.pdf.
28. Rachel Will, "Virgin Atlantic's Upper Class Onesie," *DestinAsian*, June 11, 2014, http://www.destinasian.com/blog/airline-news/virgin-atlantics-upper-class-onesie.
29. "Jacquard Enabled You Empowered," Google, https://atap.google.com/jacquard/.
30. Kevin J. Boudreau and Karim R. Lakhani, "Using the Crowd as an Innovation Partner," *Harvard Business Review*, April 2013, https://hbr.org/2013/04/using-the-crowd-as-an-innovation-partner.
31. "About the Project," MIT Center for Collective Intelligence, https://www.climatecolab.org/page/about.
32. "The Smart Zero Carbon Cities Challenge 2016," MIT Center for Collective Intelligence, https://www.climatecolab.org/contests/2016/the-smart-zero-carbon-cities-challenge.
33. "Wikipedia: About," Wikipedia, last edited April 2, 2019, 15:06, https://en.wikipedia.org/wiki/Wikipedia:About.
34. "Wikipedia: Angry Birds," Wikipedia, last edited April 9, 2019, 03:08, https://en.wikipedia.org/wiki/Angry_Birds.
35. "Upwork," Wikipedia, last edited March 20, 2019, 01:09, https://en.wikipedia.org/wiki/Upwork.
36. Brandon Butler, "The myth about how Amazon's Web service started just won't die," *Network World*, March 2, 2015, https://www.networkworld.com/article/2891297/cloud-computing/the-myth-about-how-amazon-s-web-service-started-just-won-t-die.html.
.37. Jill Jusko, "Open Innovation Tools," *Industry Week*, August 12, 2009, https://www.industryweek.com/companies-amp-executives/open-innovation-tools.
38. "YARA selects Norwegian shipbuilder VARD for zero-emission vessel Yara Birkeland," Yara, August 15, 2018, https://www.yara.com/corporate-releases/yara-selects-norwegian-shipbuilder-vard-for-zero-emission-vessel-yara-birkeland/.
39. "Rolls-Royce demonstrates world's first remotely operated commercial vessel," Rolls-Royce, June 20, 2017, https://www.rolls-royce.com/media/press-releases/2017/20-06-2017-rr-demonstrates-worlds-first-remotely-operated-commercial-vessel.aspx.

Chapter 2: Make Innovation REAL
1. Ira Kalb, "Innovation Isn't Just About Brainstorming New Ideas," *Business Insider*, July 8, 2013, https://www.businessinsider.com/innovate-or-die-a-mantra-for-every-business-2013-7.

2. Kai Ryssdal and Tommy Andres, "Domino's CEO Patrick Doyle: Tech with a side of pizza," *Marketplace*, September 24, 2015, https://www.marketplace.org/2015/09/24/business/corner-office/dominos-ceo-patrick-doyle-tech-side-pizza; Harvey Shimoff, "Inspired By Harshest Critics, Domino's Rolls New Pizza," Stratgo Marketing, January 12, 2010, https://stratgomarketing.com/2010/01/12/inspired-by-their-harshest-critics-dominos-rolls-new-pizza/; Andrew Hendricks, "Domino's Re-branding Success," *Human Creative Content*, September 10, 2014, http://humancreativecontent.com/business-and-advertising/2014/9/24/fs3fzrj02fyfsyrz6w0sn2b255ga85.

3. Joana Allamani, "How Domino's Stock Has Risen over 2000% since 2010 (DPZ, AAPL, GOOG)," Investopedia, July 19, 2018, https://www.investopedia.com/news/how-domino-stock-has-risen-over-2000-2010-dpzaaplgoog/.

4. "Who the Hell Wants to Hear Actors Talk?" Quote Investigator, November 29, 2016, https://quoteinvestigator.com/2016/11/29/actors-talk/.

5. Robert Strohmeyer, "The 7 Worst Tech Predictions of All Time," *PC World*, December 31, 2008, https://www.pcworld.com/article/155984/worst_tech_predictions.html.

6. Stephen R. Lawrence, "Great Moments in Business Forecasting," 1997, http://leeds-faculty.colorado.edu/moyes/bplan/forecast.htm.

7. Bill Murphy Jr., "7 Things to Remember When You Lose Confidence, Courtesy of Airbnb," *Inc.*, July 14, 2015, https://www.inc.com/bill-murphy-jr/7-people-turned-down-the-chance-to-invest-in-airbnb.html; Brian Chesky, "7 Rejections," Medium, July 12, 2015, https://medium.com/@bchesky/7-rejections-7d894cbaa084.

8. Dan McCarthy, "Learn the Way Leaders Encourage Innovation," The Balance Careers, November 28, 2018, https://www.thebalancecareers.com/encourage-innovation-from-employees-2275816.

9. "The Innovation Toolkit," Innovation Exchange, http://www.innovation-point.com/wp-content/uploads/2016/09/CSAA-IG-Innovation-Toolkit.pdf.

10. Soren Kaplan, "How One Insurance Firm Learned to Create an Innovation Culture," *Harvard Business Review*, August 15, 2017, https://hbr.org/2017/08/how-one-insurance-firm-learned-to-create-an-innovation-culture.

11. "The Innovation Toolkit," Innovation Exchange, http://www.innovation-point.com/wp-content/uploads/2016/09/CSAA-IG-Innovation-Toolkit.pdf.

Chapter 3: Smart vs. Stupid Innovation

1. "Marketing—the Febreze story," *The Geekrebel Blog*, March 6, 2012, http://geekrebel.com/2012/03/marketing-the-febreze-story-marketing-the-feb/; Peter Cohan, "Jurassic Park: How P&G Brought Febreze Back to Life," *Forbes*, February 19, 2012, https://www.forbes.com/sites/petercohan/2012/02/19/jurassic-park-how-pg-brought-febreze-back-to-life/#2974e8287f6d; Charles Duhigg, "How Companies Learn Your Secrets," *New York Times Magazine*, February 16, 2012, https://www.nytimes.com/2012/02/19/magazine/shopping-habits.html?_r=1&pagewanted=all&pagewanted=print.

2. "Strategies for sustained innovation," *World of an Entrepreneur* (blog), February 11, 2012, http://engineering-info-park.blogspot.com/2012/02/strategies-for-sustained-innovation.html.

3. Vijay Govindarajan and Srikanth Srinivas, "The Innovation Mindset in Action: 3M Corporation," *Harvard Business Review*, August 6, 2013, https://hbr.org/2013/08/the-innovation-mindset-in-acti-3.

4. Jana Kasperkevic, "Google Secretly Phases Out '20% Time,'" *Inc.*, August 16, 2013, https://www.inc.com/jana-kasperkevic/google-secretly-phases-out-20-percent-time.html.

5. Linda Grant, "Gillette Knows Shaving—and How to Turn Out Hot New Products," CNN Money, October 14, 1996, https://money.cnn.com/magazines/fortune/fortune_archive/1996/10/14/217832/index.htm.

6. Shona L. Brown and Kathleen M. Eisenhardt, *Competing on the Edge: Strategy as Structured Chaos* (Boston, Harvard Business School Press, 1998), 17, https://books.google.com/books?id=Q86Vr44OkwgC&pg=PA17&lpg=PA17&dq=3M,+30+percent+of+sales+must+come+from+products+less+than+four+years+old&source=bl&ots=PRMEJFCywm&sig=oVES02Le4MTWM43IquUdFcf7mJs&hl=en&sa=X&ved=2ahUKEwiE7M3iytbdAhWrg-AKHamwBtIQ6AEwAXoECAkQAQ#v=onepage&q=3M%2C%2030%20percent%20of%20sales%20must%20come%20from%20products%20less%20than%20four%20years%20old&f=false; Eric von Hippel, Stefan Thomke, and Mary Sonnack, "Creating Breakthroughs at 3M," *Harvard Business Review*, September-October 1999, https://hbr.org/1999/09/creating-breakthroughs-at-3m.

7. "John Mackey Quotes," Quotewise, http://www.quoteswise.com/john-mackey-quotes-3.html.

8. Faith Popcorn, *EVEolution: Understanding Women - 8 Essential Truths That Work In Your Business & Life*, (New York: Hyperion, 2000), https://books.google.com/books?id=ABdcDQAAQBAJ&pg=PT173&lpg=PT173&dq=Mackey+would+respond,+%E2%80%9CIf+you+accomplish+what+this+person+has+accomplished,+I%E2%80%99ll+pay+you+that,+too.%E2%80%9D&source=bl&ots=c_21V4a37r&sig=vBUN8lgMogVFBn86MSUTU_5OcHg&hl=en&sa=X&ved=2ahUKEwie8bjhy9bdAhXiYN8KHQFXANgQ6AEwAHoECAEQAQ#v=onepage&q=Mackey%20would%20respond%2C%20%E2%80%9CIf%20you%20accomplish%20what%20this%20person%20has%20accomplished%2C%20I%E2%80%99ll%20pay%20you%20that%2C%20too.%E2%80%9D&f=false; "Should You Know Your Bosses Salary?" *The Tim Sackett Project* (blog), April 30, 2014, https://timsackett.com/2014/04/30/should-you-know-your-bosses-salary/; John Bell, "Board of Directors Resolution: Pay Attention to Culture," *In the CEO Afterlife* (blog), February 20, 2015, http://www.ceoafterlife.com/uncategorized/board-of-directors-resolution-pay-attention-to-culture/.

9. Lawrence Mishel and Jessica Schieder, "CEO compensation surged in 2017," Economic Policy Institute, August 16, 2018, https://www.epi.org/publication/ceo-compensation-surged-in-2017/.

Chapter 4: The Innovation Mission

1. Nathan Bomey, "5 reasons Toys R Us failed to survive bankruptcy," *USA Today*, March 18, 2018, https://www.usatoday.com/story/money/2018/03/18/toys-r -us-bankruptcy-liquidation/436176002/; Denise Dahlhoff and Mark A. Cohen, "What Went Wrong: The Demise of Toys R Us," Knowledge @ Wharton, March 14 2018, http://knowledge.wharton.upenn.edu/article/the-demise-of-toys-r-us/; Chris Isidore, "Amazon didn't kill Toys 'R' Us. Here's what did," CNN, March 15, 2018, https://money.cnn.com/2018/03/15/news/companies/toys-r-us-closing -blame/index.html; Adam Hartung, "Toys R Us—How Bad Assumptions Fed Bad Financial Planning Creating Failure," *Forbes*, September 20, 2017, https://www .forbes.com/sites/adamhartung/2017/09/20/toys-r-us-is-a-lesson-in-how-bad -assumptions-feed-bad-financial-planning-creating-failure/#24afa0cd58ea.

2. Jessica DiNapoli and Melissa Fares, "Toys 'R' Us plans new playdate with U.S. shoppers," Reuters, December 21, 2017, https://www.reuters.com/article /us-toys-r-us-restructuring/toys-r-us-plans-new-playdate-with-u-s-shoppers -idUSKBN1EF0GD.

3. Steve Tobak, "Facebook's Mark Zuckerberg—Insights For Entrepreneurs," CBSnews, October 31, 2011, https://www.cbsnews.com/news/facebooks-mark -zuckerberg-insights-for-entrepreneurs/; Colleen Taylor, "Mark Zuckerberg To Speak Tomorrow At Y Combinator Startup School," TechCrunch, 2012, https://techcrunch.com/2012/10/19/mark-zuckerberg-2012-y-combinator-startup -school/.

4. "Chief innovation officer," Wikivividly, https://wikivividly.com/wiki/Chief _innovation_officer; William L. Miller, "Innovation for Business Growth," JSTOR, https://www.jstor.org/stable/24134057?seq=1#page_scan_tab_contents.

5. Ron Ashkenas, "Ten Ways to Inhibit Innovation," *Harvard Business Review*, July 24, 2012, https://hbr.org/2012/07/ten-ways-to-inhibit-innovation.html.

6. Roman Mica, "What if GM had not killed the electric car?" The Fast Lane Car, February 18, 2009, https://www.tflcar.com/2009/02/what-if-gm-had-not-killed -the-electic-car/.

7. "Virtual Room Designer," Lowes, https://www.lowes.com/l/virtual-room -designer.html.

8. "Family Business," Patagonia, https://www.patagonia.ca/family-business-on-site -child-care.html.

9. Rose Marcario, "Patagonia's CEO Explains How To Make On-Site Child Care Pay For Itself," *Fast Company*, August 15, 2016, https://www.fastcompany. com/3062792/patagonias-ceo-explains-how-to-make-onsite-child-care-pay-for -itself.

Chapter 5: The Six Commitments of Your Innovation Mandate

1. *The Amazon blog day one*, Amazon, https://www.aboutamazon.co.uk/innovation.

2. Will Knight, "Inside Amazon's Warehouse, Human-Robot Symbiosis," *MIT Technology Review*, July 7, 2015, https://www.technologyreview.com/s/538601 /inside-amazons-warehouse-human-robot-symbiosis/.

3. Cory Checketts, "What is Frustration-Free Packaging?" Seller Labs, May 3, 2016, https://www.sellerlabs.com/blog/what-is-frustration-free-packaging/; Lisa McTigue Pierce, "Amazon incentivizes brands to create Frustration-Free Packaging," *Packaging Digest*, September 18, 2018, https://www.packagingdigest.com/sustainable-packaging/amazon-incentivizes-brands-to-create-frustration-free-packaging-2018-09-18.

4. "Amazon Patents," Justia Patents, https://patents.justia.com/company/amazon; Timothy B. Lee, "How Amazon innovates in ways that Google and Apple can't," Vox, December 28, 2016, https://www.vox.com/new-money/2016/12/28/13889840/amazon-innovation-google-apple; Keary Crawford, "Amazon Innovates with Its Business Model, Not Drones," *Wired*, https://www.wired.com/insights/2014/01/amazon-innovates-business-model-drones/; Greg Satell, "How Amazon Innovates," *Inc.*, September 23, 2018, https://www.inc.com/greg-satell/the-secret-behind-amazons-uncanny-ability-to-out-innovate-just-about-every-other-company-on-planet.html.

5. Lola Butcher, "Investing in Innovation to Disrupt Health Care's Status Quo," Hospitals and Health Systems Network, September 15, 2015, https://www.hhnmag.com/articles/3214-investing-in-innovation-to-disrupt-health-cares-status-quo.

6. "Destinations—KAYAK Hack Week Project 2012," *mpv's little blog*, February 11, 2013, http://blog.mikevosseller.com/2013/02/destinations-kayak-hack-week-project.html; Aaron Lester, "More companies include retreat time to innovate," *Boston Globe*, December 7, 2012, https://www.bostonglobe.com/business/2012/12/07/companies-set-aside-time-for-employees-innovate/Y4cWITyVjmpvKhOfV0GQiM/story.html.

7. "ShipIt," Atlassian, https://www.atlassian.com/company/shipit.

8. Christina Chaey, "LinkedIn Launches An Incubator To Turn Employees Into Entrepreneurs," *Fast Company*, December 12, 2012, https://www.fastcompany.com/3003818/linkedin-launches-incubator-turn-employees-entrepreneurs; Kevin Scott, "The LinkedIn [in]cubator," *the LinkedIn Official blog*, December 7, 2012, https://blog.linkedin.com/2012/12/07/linkedin-incubator.

9. Barry Jaruzelski, Volker Staack, and Kevin Schwartz, "Innovation's New World Order," October 2015, https://www.strategyand.pwc.com/media/file/2015-Global-Innovation-1000-Fact-Pack.pdf;

10 Michael Casey and Robert Hackett, "The 10 biggest R&D spenders worldwide," *Fortune*, November 17, 2014, http://fortune.com/2014/11/17/top-10-research-development/.

11. "Google its challenges in rd and how it manages them," Course Hero, https://www.coursehero.com/file/p2buqq3/Google-its-challenges-in-RD-and-how-it-manages-them-Google-has-invested/.

12. "PwC's Innovation Benchmark Report," PwC, https://www.pwc.com/us/en/services/consulting/innovation-benchmark-findings.html.

13. Tamsin Oxford, "Investing in innovation," *Brainstorm*, March 28, 2017, http://www.brainstormmag.co.za/innovation/12808-investing-in-innovation.

14. Kat Boogaard, "20 Companies That Value Learning," The Muse, https://www.themuse.com/advice/20-companies-that-value-learning; "Professional Development," Health Care Service Corporation, http://www.hcsc .com/careers/total-rewards/professional-development.html.

15. Claire Zillman, "These 6 Companies Give Their Employees Unlimited Tuition Reimbursement," *Fortune*, March 4, 2016, http://fortune.com/2016/03/04 /companies-employees-tuition-reimbursement/.

16. Joe Iarocci, "14 Servant Leadership Beliefs of TDIndustries," Cairnway Center, March 14, 2016, https://serveleadnow.com/14-servant-leadership-beliefs-of -tdindustries/.

17. "Millennials Desperate for Financial Stability, In Search of Employer Support to Get There," EdAssist, https://www.edassist.com/resources/news-releases/2015/04 /millennials-study-press.

18. Lauren Lee, "Hack Week is here," *Work in Progress* (blog), August 17, 2015, https://blogs.dropbox.com/dropbox/2015/08/hack-week-2015/.

19. Gerald C. Kane and Anh Nguyen (interviewers), "Cultivating a Culture of Cross-Functional Teaming and Learning at CarMax," *MIT Sloan Management Review*, August 11, 2017, https://sloanreview.mit.edu/article/cultivating-a-culture-of-cross -functional-teaming-and-learning-at-carmax/.

20. John C. Maxwell Quotes, BrainyQuote, https://www.brainyquote.com/quotes /john_c_maxwell_600862.

21. Timothy Gubler, Ian Larkin, and Lamar Pierce, "The Dirty Laundry of Employee Award Programs: Evidence from the Field," Harvard Business School, February 11, 2013, https://www.hbs.edu/faculty/Publication%20Files/13-069_72eed050 -c2d7-4dc1-9f32-f773cc108fde.pdf.

22. Saktipada Maity, "Capgemini Consulting and Altimeter global report reveals leading businesses continue to struggle with innovation, with traditional R&D model 'broken,'" Capgemini, July 23, 2015, https://www.capgemini.com/news /capgemini-consulting-and-altimeter-global-report-reveals-leading-businesses -continue-to/.

23. Lab1886. The global innovation machine, Daimler, https://www.daimler.com /innovation/venture/lab1886-en.html.

24. Jennifer Valentino-DeVries, "Steve Jobs's Best Quotes," *Wall Street Journal*, August 24, 2011, https://blogs.wsj.com/digits/2011/08/24/steve-jobss-best-quotes/.

25. Thomas J. DeLong and Vineeta Vijayaraghavan, "Case Study: Should You Listen to the Customer?" *Harvard Business Review*, June 13, 2012, https://hbr.org/2012/06/case-study-should-you-listen-t.

26. Blaise Zerega, "Open Bar for Beta Testers," *New Yorker*, April 30, 2018, https://www.newyorker.com/magazine/2018/04/30/an-open-bar-for-beta-testers.

Chapter 6: The Whole Enchilada

1. Adi Alon, Wouter Koetzier, Steve Culp, "The Art of Managing Innovation Risk," Accenture, https://www.accenture.com/us-en/insight-outlook-art-of-managing -innovation-risk.

2. Emma Carter, "Why Your Company Should Adopt Innovation Days," ThoughtWorks, January 5, 2016, https://www.thoughtworks.com/insights/blog/why-your-company-should-adopt-innovation-days.

3. Gary L. Neilson, Karla L. Martin, and Elizabeth Powers, "The Secrets to Successful Strategy Execution," *Harvard Business Review*, June 2008, https://hbr.org/2008/06/the-secrets-to-successful-strategy-execution.

4. Dan Silvestre, "Steve Jobs Insane Productivity Secrets," The Startup, September 7, https://medium.com/swlh/steve-jobs-insane-productivity-secrets-470e99c482f6; Jason Fell, "How Steve Jobs Saved Apple," *Entrepreneur*, October 27, 2011, https://www.entrepreneur.com/article/220604.

5. John Tamny, "Walter Isaacson's 'Steve Jobs' Is a Great Lesson In Economics," *Forbes*, November 13, 2012, https://www.forbes.com/sites/johntamny/2012/11/13/walter-isaacsons-steve-jobs-is-a-great-lesson-in-economics/#1859f11b728b.

6. https://techcrunch.com/tag/tiny-speck/, Tiny Speck; "Slack Technologies," Wikipedia, last edited March 29, 2019, 9:20 https://en.wikipedia.org/wiki/Slack_Technologies; https://www.giantbomb.com/tiny-speck/3010-7665/.

Chapter 7: Systems = Good, Chaos = Bad
1. "Initial Franchising Costs with 7-Eleven," *Entrepreneur*, November 21, 2018, http://franchise.7-eleven.com/franchise-blog/initial-franchising-costs-with-7-eleven; https://www.entrepreneur.com/franchises/7elevenInc/282052.

2. Andrea Gabor, "Seeing Your Company as a System," strategy+business, May 25, 2010, https://www.strategy-business.com/article/10210?gko=20cca.

3. Michael Porter, "Truck Accident Lawyer," Consumer Safety, https://www.consumersafety.org/safety/gm-ignition-switches/; Max Blau, "No Accident: Inside GM's deadly ignition switch scandal," *Atlanta*, January 6, 2016, https://www.atlantamagazine.com/great-reads/no-accident-inside-gms-deadly-ignition-switch-scandal/; "General Motors ignition switch recalls," Wikipedia, last edited March 5 2019, 19:24, https://en.wikipedia.org/wiki/General_Motors_ignition_switch_recalls.

4. "ANA Quality and Innovation Conference—Sharing innovations and advice," American Nurses Association, March 23, 2018, https://www.nursingworld.org/news/news-releases/2018/ana-quality-and-innovation-conference---sharing-innovations-and-advice/.

5. "ANA Quality and Innovation Conference—Sharing Innovations and advice."

Chapter 8: The Innovation Operating System (IOS)
1. Axelle Tessandier, "The New Explorers," *Huffington Post*, January 23, 2014, https://www.huffingtonpost.com/axelle-tessandier/the-new-explorers_b_4275782.html.

2. Polly Mosendz, "Microsoft's CEO Sent a 3,187-Word Memo and We Read it So You Don't Have To," *The Atlantic*, July 10, 2014, https://www.theatlantic.com/technology/archive/2014/07/microsofts-ceo-sent-a-3187-word-memo-and-we-read-it-so-you-dont-have-to/374230/.

3. "Leadership Quotes from Jack Welch," Leadership & Ethics Institute, July 17, 2012, http://gwclei.com/leadership-quotes-from-jack-welch/.

4. "Best Examples of Company Vision and Mission Statements," Blender, https://www.themarketingblender.com/vision-mission-statements/; "100+ of the World's Best Vision Statements," Cascade, https://www.executestrategy.net/wp -content/uploads/2016/06/100-of-the-worlds-best-vision-statements.pdf.

5. "The Innovation Gap," Korn Ferry Institute, https://www.kornferry.com/institute /download/view/id/17450/aid/1089.

6. Linus Torvalds, August 25, 1991, https://groups.google.com/forum/#!original /comp.os.minix/dlNtH7RRrGA/SwRavCzVE7gJ.

7. Tim Burke, "Community collaboration at scale: The quarter-century evolution of the Linux project," *Red Hat Blog*, August 25, 2016, https://www.redhat.com/en /blog/community-collaboration-scale-quarter-century-evolution-linux-project.

8. The Linux Foundation, https://www.linuxfoundation.org/about/.

Chapter 9: The Innovation Pipeline

1. Eiji Toyoda, "Good Thinking, Good Products," May 2005, https://www.toyota-global. com/company/toyota_traditions/quality/may_jun_2005.html (page discontinued).

2. Keshia Hannam, "'Hamilton' Investors Have Seen Returns of Over 600% on the Hip Hop Musical," *Fortune*, December 21, 2017, http://fortune.com/2017/12/21 /hamilton-investors-unprecedented-returns/.

3. Henry Chesbrough, *Open Innovation: The New Imperative for Creating and Profiting from Technology* (Boston, Harvard Business Review Press, 2005), https://www.amazon.com/Open-Innovation-Imperative-Profiting-Technology /dp/1422102831.

4. Molly St. Louis, "How to Channel Feedback into an Impactful Innovation," *Inc.*, March 27, 2017, https://www.inc.com/molly-reynolds/how-to-channel-feedback -into-an-impactful-innovation.html.

5. James Estrin, "Kodak's First Digital Moment," *New York Times*, August 12, 2015, https://lens.blogs.nytimes.com/2015/08/12/kodaks-first-digital-moment/.

6. Peter Ha, "Apple QuickTake 100," *Time*, October 25, 2010, http://content.time. com/time/specials/packages/article/0,28804,2023689_2023773_2023615,00.html.

7. Jackie Hunter, "Collaboration For Innovation Is The New Mantra For The Pharmaceutical Industry," DDW, Spring 2014, https://www.ddw-online.com /business/p217613-collaboration-for-innovation-is-the-new-mantra-for-the -pharmaceutical-industry-spring-14.html. Access to the Pfizer website was blocked by my browser as "unsafe."

8. Owen Edwards, "The Death of the EV-1," *Smithsonian*, June 2006, https://www .smithsonianmag.com/science-nature/the-death-of-the-ev-1-118595941/.

9. "In Walt's Own Words: Plussing Disneyland," *Walt Disney blog*, July 17, 2014, https://www.waltdisney.org/blog/walts-own-words-plussing-disneyland.

10. Trevor Datson, "Coca-Cola Admits That Dasani is Nothing But Tap Water," Common Dreams, March 4, 2004, https://www.commondreams.org/dasani -nothing-but-tap-water.

11. "The birth of movie merchandising," University of California, http://ucresearch
    .tumblr.com/post/88958238676/the-birth-of-movie-merchandising-the-lost.

12. Bernard Weinraub, "Selling 'Jurassic': The Film And Toys," *New York Times*, June
    14, 1993, https://www.nytimes.com/1993/06/14/movies/selling-jurassic-the-film
    -and-toys.html.

13. Mansoor Mithaiwala, "*Black Panther* Pushes MCU Past $14 Billion Globally,"
    ScreenRant, February 23, 2018, https://screenrant.com/black-panther-mcu
    -billion-gross/.

14. Esty, Benjamin, "Bankruptcy and Restructuring at Marvel Entertainment
    Group," Harvard Business School, https://www.hbs.edu/faculty/Pages/item.
    aspx?num=8013.

15. Sean Cole, "How Nike uses Facebook and Instagram," *Econsultancy* (blog),
    December 5, 2018, https://econsultancy.com/how-nike-uses-facebook-twitter
    -pinterest-and-google/.

16. "The Candle Problem From 1945 Is a Logic Puzzle That Requires Creative
    Thinking," Curiosity, https://curiosity.com/topics/the-candle-problem-from-1945
    -is-a-logic-puzzle-that-requires-creative-thinking-curiosity/.

17. Lori Castle, "The Art of Innovation," Consumer Goods Technology, March 3,
    2008, https://consumergoods.com/art-innovation; "Universe of Innovation,"
    Crayola, https://www.crayola.com/inspiration-galleries/visual-voices-2010
    /universe-of-innovation/; Robert Klara, "How Crayola Crayons Gave Its
    Century-Old Product Renewed Relevance in the Age of iPads," *Adweek*,
    September 5, 2017, https://www.adweek.com/brand-marketing/crayola-has
    -given-its-century-old-product-a-contemporary-relevance-even-in-the-age-of
    -ipads/.

Chapter 10: The Innovation Brand Plan

1. "Bring In the Brains: How to Hire Innovators," Business, February 22, 2017,
   https://www.business.com/articles/bring-in-the-brains-how-to-hire-innovators/.

2. Kickstarter, https://www.kickstarter.com/about.

3. Kristin Kloberdanz, "Working The Crowd: This Fuse Will Set The Collective
   Brain On Fire," GE Reports, April 28, 2017, https://www.ge.com/reports
   /working-crowd-fuse-will-set-collective-brain-fire/.

4. "The Millennial Survey 2014," Deloitte, https://www2.deloitte.com/al/en/pages
   /about-deloitte/articles/2014-millennial-survey-positive-impact.html.

5. Joann Muller, "May Mobility Is Deploying Self-Driving Vehicles Now, Starting In
   Detroit," *Forbes*, June 26, 2018, https://www.forbes.com/sites
   /joannmuller/2018/06/26/may-mobility-is-deploying-self-driving-vehicles-block
   -by-block-starting-in-detroit/.

6. Darrell Etherington, "May Mobility is a self-driving startup with a decade of
   experience," TechCrunch, https://techcrunch.com/2017/08/21/may-mobility-is-a
   -self-driving-startup-with-a-decade-of-experience/.

7. Darrell Etherington, "May Mobility is a self-driving startup with a decade of
   experience."

Chapter 11: Long-Term Innovation Success

1. Emily Tamkin, "Keeping It in the Family," *Slate*, October 20, 2014, http://www.slate.com/articles/business/continuously_operating/2014/10/world_s_oldest_companies_why_are_so_many_of_them_in_japan.html; "List of oldest companies," Wikipedia, last edited April 2, 2019, 13:26, https://en.wikipedia.org/wiki/List_of_oldest_companies.

2. Maxwell Wessel, "Big Companies Can't Innovate Halfway," *Harvard Business Review*, October 4, 2012, https://hbr.org/2012/10/big-companies-cant-innovate-halfway.

3. "PARC (company)," Wikipedia, last edited March 7, 2019, 05:07, https://en.wikipedia.org/wiki/PARC_(company); parc, https://www.parc.com/; "The Xerox PARC Visit," Stanford University, https://web.stanford.edu/dept/SUL/sites/mac/parc.html.

4. "World's Most Innovative Companies," *Forbes*, June 6, 2018, https://www.forbes.com/companies/servicenow/?list=innovative-companies#34744d17529e.

5. Meghan Lockwood, "Why Service Now (Really is) More Innovative Than Tesla," Acorio, May 31, 2018, https://www.acorio.com/servicenow-most-innovative-company-world/.

6. Kathleen Chaykowski and Mark Coatney, "From Broke To Billionaire: How Fred Luddy Built The World's Most Innovative Company," *Forbes*, May 29, 2018, https://www.forbes.com/feature/innovative-companies-service-now/#1e39ecbfc603.

7. Kathleen Chaykowski and Mark Coatney, "From Broke To Billionaire."

INDEX

ABOUT THE AUTHOR

As one of the world's leading innovation strategists and futurists, Nicholas J. Webb, CEO of LeaderLogic, works closely with Fortune 500 companies throughout the world to help them lead their industries in innovation, strategy, and growth. He serves as Chief Innovation Officer for the Center for Innovation at Western University of Health Sciences in Pomona, California, and is an adjunct professor of health sciences. He speaks at 50+ events annually, and his clients include Gatorade, CIGNA, Freightliner, Johnson & Johnson, Verizon Wireless, Salesforce, Siemens, FedEx, and Genetech. Webb has been awarded more than 40 patents by the US patent and trademark office, for medical, industrial, and consumer technologies.